Inside...

186 PAGES
of step-by-step guidance
Leading you through the major procedures on most types of bicycle

PLUS!
Scores of specialist tips and loads of inside workshop information

bicycle maintenance 3

Foreword

Cycle maintenance is critical for every bike rider, and whether you're a professional like myself or a beginner to the track, road or trail, it's crucial to take it seriously. As a professional I need my bike in perfect condition every day, because if a part fails and I can't train, it will have a detrimental effect on my race performance.

Winter is the worst season for keeping your bike in working order. There is usually a lot of rain, salt and rubbish on the roads which will quickly find their way into small nuts and bolts, slowly eroding the components of your bike. After training, I always give mine a quick wash and check over to stay on top of everything – I highly recommend you do the same.

Knowing your way around your bike is the key to successfully maintaining it. We have lots of mechanics at our base in Manchester and at all the races/training camps we attend, but I personally ensure I check the brake pads and tyres before every outing.

Whatever your skill or experience, regular maintenance is the best way of getting the most from your bike, and this excellent guide will help you do just that.

Happy riding!

Geraint Thomas MBE

Olympic gold medalist and rider for Team Sky

Contributors

Writers Guy Andrews and Stuart Clapp
Editor Tym Manley
Principal photographer Gerard Brown
Additional photography Danny Bird
MagBook Design Nick Watts and Anand Parmar
Digital Production Manager Nicky Baker
Advertising Chris Brown

Management

MagBook Publisher Dharmesh Mistry
Production Director Robin Ryan
MD of Advertising Julian Lloyd-Evans
Newstrade Director David Barker
Commercial & Retail Director Martin Belson
Chief Financial Officer Brett Reynolds
Group Finance Director Ian Leggett
Chief Executive James Tye
Chairman Felix Dennis

MAGBOOK

Licensing
To license this product please contact Carlotta Serantoni on +44 (0) 20 79076550 or email carlotta_serantoni@dennis.co.uk
To syndicate content from this product please contact Anj Dosaj Halai on +44(0) 20 7907 6132 or email anj_dosaj-halai@dennis.co.uk

Thanks to Evans Cycles for their help with the cover shoot.

Welcome

The main reason you're reading this is because you have discovered what a peerless machine the bicycle is, bringing you excitement and pleasure while keeping you fit and saving both your money and your planet.

The other reason you're here is because you have also discovered that all types of bicycle eventually succumb to wear and tear.

Not so often really, considering that, to satisfy your need for excitement and maximum efficiency the bicycle not only has to be both light and finely engineered but spend its time carrying your weight through thick and thin while the most powerful muscles in your body stamp down on it with extreme prejudice. Still, go wrong they will, particularly if just ridden until something goes 'graunch'.

Prevention is better than cure...
The best way to avoid any unpleasantness is to care for your bike regularly, cleaning it, checking it for early signs of wear and replacing or upgrading components as you need to. The Ultimate Guide takes you through the main procedures for the most popular types of bicycle.

BIKE MAP
Drive Side

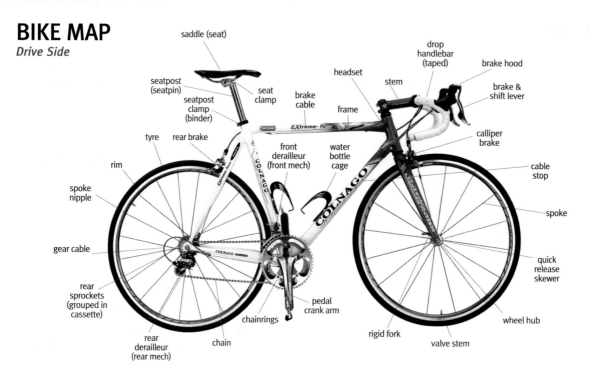

saddle (seat)

drop handlebar (taped)

brake hood

seatpost (seatpin)

headset

stem

brake & shift lever

seatpost clamp (binder)

seat clamp

brake cable

frame

tyre

rear brake

calliper brake

rim

front derailleur (front mech)

water bottle cage

cable stop

spoke nipple

spoke

gear cable

quick release skewer

rear sprockets (grouped in cassette)

pedal crank arm

chainrings

wheel hub

rear derailleur (rear mech)

chain

rigid fork

valve stem

BIKE MAP
Opposite Drive Side

grips

gear shifter

handlebars (riser)

shock (for rear suspension)

brake lever

handlebar stem (short, rising)

aheadset

suspension pivots

suspension forks

brake hose (hydraulic)

disc brake callipers

brake disc (rotor)

THE 'M' CHECK

The basic safety inspection of a bike is referred to as the 'M' check (because of the path it takes along the bike). Ensuring your bike is set up correctly, this easy examination takes minutes to complete, and is very handy for beginners. Take time to perform the 'M' check to spot problems with components before they fail.

Rear/Front Wheel:

- Check the quick releases and wheel nuts are secure. For quick release skewers, the front should point vertically alongside the fork, while the rear should be horizontal between the seat and chain stays or tucked beneath the chain stay if this isn't possible.
- Check that the wheels are true by rotating while checking spokes for anomalies, indicating they may be bent or loose.
- Check the wheel for defects in the hub, the wheel should spin freely.
- Check the tyre for any cuts or obvious signs of wear.
- Check that the tyre is inflated to the optimum PSI. Too little air and there is a risk of getting a pinch flat.

Rear Derailleur:

- Check that the gears are indexing correctly by shifting a gear at a time, lifting the rear wheel and rotating the pedals.
- Check for alignment; be sure that when checking the indexing, the rear derailleur isn't touching the spokes.

Rear Brake:

- Check that the brake is working effectively by holding the lever and pulling the bike backwards.
- Check that brake blocks are fitted correctly and haven't worn unevenly or beyond their wear indicators.
- Check the brake cables for signs of rust.

Saddle:

- Check that the saddle is at optimum height.
- Check the saddle is level and straight by lining it up with the top tube.
- Check the seat pin to make sure the 'minimum insertion' stamp is well within the seat tube. Ensure the seat pin is firmly in place.

Front Derailleur:

- Check that the mechanism is shifting the chain onto the chain rings, not overshooting and dropping the chain.
- Check that the cable is secure and has no signs of rust or fraying.

Chain:

- Check the chain for rust.
- Check that the chain is lubed.
- Check the chain for sticky links and assure it runs smoothly around the chainrings.

Handlebars:

- Check the headset bearings by applying the brakes and rocking the bike backwards and forwards. Look out for play within the headset, this indicates a fault.
- Check that the bars turn freely and easily.
- Check that the handlebars are aligned, centered and securely held in position by the stem.

Stems:

- Check that the stem is aligned by gripping the front wheel with your knees and lining the stem with the wheel.
- Check that quill stems aren't showing the minimum insertion marker above the head tube.

Headset:

- Check the headset bearings by applying the brakes and rocking the bike backwards and forwards. Look out for play within the headset, this indicates a fault.

Levers:

- Check that the brake levers are within easy reach.
- Check that gear levers shift correctly.

Accessories:

- Check all fixings are firmly in place and do not obscure moving parts
- Check batteries/power for lights.

UPGRADE...
Rim Tape
Inspect your rim tape occasionally for signs of wear; this could be the reason for those persistent punctures.

Cleaning & Maintenance

Cleaning a bike extends its life and you catch faults early

No matter how determined you are to keep your bikes in top condition yourself, you may feel you need a bit of experience before, say, changing a bottom bracket bearing. That's good sense. But general maintenance is something anyone can do if they have this book and the tools. There are also some running repairs it's essential to be able to do out on a ride unless you want a long walk home. This section discusses the tools you need in the workshop for upgrading and general maintenance and those to take out on the trail for emergency repair. Also, top of the list under the heading maintenance comes washing and lubricating the bike. Regular cleaning, done right, increases the life of every

component and it's while doing it that you find the frayed cables, the dents and dings and even, heaven forbid, the cracks of doom. Wash your road bikes once a week and mountain bikes after every ride, unless it is extraordinarily dry. It's far easier while the mud's still wet anyway...

"Regular cleaning, done right, increases the life of every component"

Overdoing it

Yes you can clean too much. Power hoses blast the mud and traffic film off very well; they also strip the lube from every surface and drive the grease out of the bearings. If you have the time, the bucket, brush and sponge combination is still the safest method. For the same reasons, powerful de-greasers also need care; it's wise to dilute them.

The home workshop

A modest outlay on tools will cover most home workshop jobs. Specialist tools are more expensive though, so it may pay to let your local bike shop do the big stuff while you build the confidence to take the plunge...

This is the basic set of home workshop tools that will cover most of your needs:

- Allen keys – 1.5, 2, 2.5, 3, 4, 5, 6, 8 and 10 mm are the sizes most often used
- track pump
- chain cleaner
- cleaning brushes
- pliers (flat and needle nose)
- cable cutters
- screwdrivers (small and large; flat and cross-head)
- nylon hammer (or mallet) and ball-peen (metalworking) hammer
- a set of metric, open-ended spanners from 6 mm to 24 mm
- cassette lock ring tool
- chain whip
- chain tool
- cable puller
- 'podger' sharp-ended tool like a bradawl
- star nut-setting tool
- adjustable spanner
- cone spanners (17 mm, 15 mm and 13 mm)
- pedal spanner
- workshop quality chain tool chain checker (for measuring chain wear)
- torque wrenches
- crank-removing tool
- bottom bracket tools
- headset spanners (optional)
- wheel-truing stand, spoke keys

You may also find the following items useful:

- disc brake bleed kit
- hacksaw (standard and junior)
- files
- socket set

Advanced workshop tools
As you become more experienced, add the following items to your workshop tool kit:

- headset press
- headset cup remover
- crown race remover
- crown race setting tool
- rear derailleur hanger straightening tool
- set of taps for threads
- rear dropout alignment tools
- disc brake facing kit
- steerer cutting guide.

Pro Workshop Tools
- head tube reamer and facing kit
- bottom bracket tapping and facing kit
- fork crown facing kit
- seat tube reamer
- frame alignment tool
- chainline gauge
- wheel dishing stick
- spoke tension meter

On the bike tool kit

Your basic kit should contain a folding set of Allen keys, a screwdriver, two tyre levers, a tube or two and a set of emergency patches. A saddle pack will carry the basic kit so you won't have to fill your pockets with tools. For longer rides, you might want to add a chain tool, a spoke key, a small spanner and some minor spares, such as brake pads and chain links.

- tyre levers
- two spare tubes
- puncture kit or emergency patches
- tyre boot
- spoke key and spare spoke (cable spokes are good for emergencies)
- a good pump that can double up as a shock pump (if you have air forks or rear suspension)
- a quality chain tool and a few spare links and pins

- Allen keys – usually 2.5, 3, 4, 5, 6 and 8 mm
- Leatherman-style multi-tool with pliers and a sharp knife
- small dropper bottle of chain oil
- zip ties
- spare cables and brake pads (only really essential if you are miles from a bike shop)

UPGRADE...
Bottle Cages
Fluids are essential for any length of ride. There are styles of bottle cages to suit every bike - stay hydrated!

Mountain bikers find hydration-type rucksacks ideal for carrying more kit, especially the bulky items like inner tubes and shock pump. It's better to carry this stuff on your back, away from your bike but also away from your pockets, which can become saggy and annoying when you're hopping the bike over obstacles.

Trail tool tips

✔ Spokes can be taped to a frame tube or hidden in the seatpost.

✔ Cable spokes are handy for quick repairs and, as they hook into the spoke holes rather than having to be pushed through, you don't have to remove the cassette to repair it.

✔ Always leave your trail tool kit intact and keep it just for riding. Taking tools out to fix your bike at home will mean you'll leave your tyre levers on the kitchen table and not have them with you when you really need them...

✔ Carry a spoke key on your key ring – this makes your keys easier to find too!

✔ Tool kits can be stuffed into old drink bottles and placed in a spare bottle cage. Make sure it can't rattle out by securing it with a toe strap.

✔ If you are riding with friends, there's no need to double up on shock and tyre pumps. Spread the tools around so you're not all carrying the same stuff.

Workshop setup

A home workshop is a bit of a luxury, but fixing your bike in the kitchen is never a great idea. So here are some bike storage ideas and tips for setting up your workshop at home.

1. A stable work stand is essential. The best workshop type will be fixed to a wall or a solid workbench, so jobs that

require bashing or heavy leaning won't make the stand move around the floor as you 'dance' with your bike.

2. Put down a mat for spillage. Remember that if you have to fix your bike in the kitchen, you will need something on the floor to soak up the mess. Workshop mats are readily available from bike or tool shops. They also keep your feet warm in the winter.

3. Hooks and lockable anchor points are a good idea, just in case you are broken into. Storing your bike(s) like this also prevents them from falling over and getting scratched by the lawn mower.

4. A solid workbench makes tough jobs like fitting headset parts or cutting down fork steerers easy. A tool board helps you find tools quickly, and quality tools should be stored in a tool box if your workshop is damp. You can also assemble a field tool box that you can take with you to races or trail rides so you can fix emergencies in the car park.

5. The vice needs to be properly bolted and secured to the solid workbench. A vice is essential for hub and headset jobs, and a pair of replaceable 'soft jaws' for the vice

will help to protect valuable and sensitive components.

6. An electric drill will help with frame repairs and removing seized SPD bolts, and a bench-mounted grinder is useful for repairs and

customising components, but care must be taken when working to wear the right protective equipment.

7. Torque wrenches take the guesswork out of assembling aeroplanes, car engines and machines, and enable engineers to fasten bolts to manufacturers' recommended figures. This type is simple to use – set the level on the screw gauge on the handle shown in Newton metres (Nm), then add the correct Allen or bolt head (they have either a 3/8 inch or a 1/4 inch socket drive) and tighten the bolt until the handle 'gives' with a click. This type is perfect for most Allen bolts on a bike.

8. Park Tool's version of a torque wrench has a beam, which 'bends' when the handle is balanced, allowing you to read off the torque on the dial. You'll need a bigger one like this for cassette lock rings, cranks and bottom brackets. On mountain bikes it is critical to use recommended torque settings, for warranty reasons and for safety – especially on suspension forks and disc brakes with many moving parts and fastenings. All well-trained mechanics will use a torque wrench – don't build a bike up without one.

9. Mountain bike tyres have a large volume and take a lot of air, so a track pump will set tyre pressures quickly and accurately and is far better than a mini pump. However, some pressure gauges are more reliable than others, so get a separate accurate tyre-pressure gauge too.

11. You will develop preferences for particular brands of lubes and greases, but the modern bicycle requires a selection of advanced lubricants to keep it running sweetly:

- ti prep (or copper slip) – a grease with tiny copper flakes in it, which prevents titanium and alloys from seizing; this must be used on all titanium threads;
- anti-seize grease – this is for large threads and components that stay put for long periods (seatposts,

bottom bracket threads, headset cups and pedal threads);
- PTFE (Teflon)-based light dry lube – this is preferred for summer use and assemblies like derailleurs and brake calliper pivots;
- heavy wet lube – this is best for wet weather as it's harder to wash away than dry lube;
- silicone greases – use these for intricate moving parts like pedal and hub bearings;
- waterproof greases – use these for components that get ignored for long periods like Aheadset bearings;
- de-greaser – used for cleaning moving parts and components that get bunged up with muck;
- bike wash – this speaks for itself; use it for tyres, frame tubes and saddles;
- release agent – this is good for removing seized seatposts and stubborn bottom brackets. Be careful as it can ruin your paintwork, and your skin.

Washing and caring for your bike

Regular cleaning helps your bike last longer. All bicycles are cleaned in much the same way, but we're demonstrating on a mountain bike because they catch most muck...

To keep your bike running smoothly and ensure that the components will last, wash your bike at least once a week – especially in the winter. Washing your bike is a great way to get close to it and inspect every aspect of its workings. Water gets into everything and therefore into all the sensitive parts of your bike, so it's best to wash your bike with care. Wear some wellies, rubber gloves and waterproof clothing, as you will then be able to concentrate on the job properly. Pressure (jet) washers are certainly quick, but are also lazy and generally not a good idea for cleaning your bike as they tend to blow water into sealed units such as the headsets, forks, hubs and bottom brackets.

They also ruin your cables and blow all the lubricant off your chain. Worse still, with complicated full suspension linkages, which can easily be neglected, the water will quickly turn bearings to rust and seize up your pivots and bushings. So, it's far better to hand-wash your bike with a sponge and brush; this way your bike will last longer and perform better. Find a suitable area to clean your bike. Be aware that you will need plenty of water and that the by-products from a mountain bike can be quite messy. Therefore, a concrete area with a water supply and a drain is best. Always clean the floor with a stiff brush when you have finished as the de-greasing fluids can make the floor very slippery.

Cleaning tools:
- water
- bucket
- brushes (large to toothbrush size)
- portable workstand
- spray-on bike wash
- strong de-greaser (citrus ones are good) for drivetrain parts
- sponge
- chain-cleaning device
- sprocket cleaner (narrow brush to get between gaps)

1 Always clean the underside of the saddle and the seatpost first. This is so you can place the bike into the work stand before you wash the rest of your bike (most work stand clamps hold the seatpost) and also because it's best to start at the top of the bike and work down, so you don't get muck on stuff you have already washed.

2 Use a brush and a sponge to get the worst of the mud off. If you are using a hosepipe, it's best to do this while the bike is still wet – once the mud is dry it gets far harder to shift. If you have space in your car, take your washing kit and a jerry can of water with you when you travel to the trails or races, so you can wash your bike before the dirt has a chance to do any damage.

3 Remove both of the wheels as they are far easier to clean when they are out of the bike. This will also give you access to the inside of the rear triangle and swing-arm mechanism, and will allow you to swing the bike around easily in the workstand.

4 Place a chain guide in the drop-out and wrap the chain over it. This will help you clean the bike and chain, let you rotate the chain and cranks easily and keep the chain out of the way as you wash the rest of the bike.

5 Place your bike in a stand at a suitable height, so you can wash the bike without bending down too much. Soak the loose mud off first, then cover your bike in bike-washing fluid. Leave this to soak in for a few moments.

6 Use a spray-on de-greaser. You can dilute these cleaning sprays as they tend to be quite concentrated and powerful, and can even go 50:50 with many of them. Be careful to read the instructions as these fluids can be caustic and affect the finish of your bike. Most are not too kind to your hands either, so it's best to wear rubber gloves.

7 Wash the tyres and use a stiff brush to knock the mud out of the tread. If you have V-brakes, pay particular attention to the rims, clean off all the black brake crud and inspect the rims for wear. Use an alcohol-based disc brake cleaning fluid on the rotors and be careful not to spread grease from any brushes you may have used on the cassette. This will contaminate the rotor or the pads and give you plenty of braking problems the next time you ride.

8 Be careful when cleaning the forks – don't spray de-greaser directly at the seals, and clean them with a sponge rather than a stiff brush. Spraying water and de-greaser into the fork internals will cause problems in the future.

UPGRADE...
Locking Grips for MTB
Applying locking grips prevents slippage and is the simplest and cheapest way to improve MTB handling

9 Rear suspension systems can collect a lot of mud. If you don't clean off the mud, it can corrode and seize the pivots. Inspect the shock for leaks and signs of wear and tear.

10 Also take special care when cleaning disc brakes, as they can become contaminated with dirty oil and lubricant residue from the drivetrain. Use a clean brush and water to clean off the discs. With V-brakes you need to remove all the crud from the pads and inspect them for grit, which may have got stuck in the slots in the pad and need to be prised out. Inspect the rims for grooves where there may be wear from the pads.

11 Clean out the pedals and the shoe cleats using a toothbrush-sized brush. Pay special attention to the cleats if you have been walking a lot on your muddy rides, as impacted mud will make the cleats malfunction. Knock the mud out or prise it out with a screwdriver as the cleats need to be clean to work properly. Keep the pedal springs well lubricated and check their tension regularly.

12 Clean all the muck out of the sprockets with a suitable implement. There are such things as sprocket cleaners, but you can just use a stiff brush. It is very important to keep the cassette clean, so sometimes it's worth removing it and giving it a thorough clean. You can then clean and inspect the hubs too.

Pro tips

✔ If you are riding in really muddy conditions, spray the frame and drivetrain with extra spray lube. This will prevent the mud from sticking so much and means you can ride for a little longer before having to stop. Be careful not to contaminate the disc pads when doing this.

✔ Use 1-inch strips of fabric to clean between the sprockets. T-shirt neck hems (the folded over bits) are particularly good for this job.

✔ If you have to use a jet wash, use it for the tyres, saddle and frame only. Wash the rest of the bike by hand.

✔ Use a bike-wash detergent on all but the really stubborn muck. You can use car shampoo or washing-up liquid, but be careful as this can be corrosive and damage the paintwork. The concentrated and stronger de-greasers (usually the citrus type) are best saved for the chains, chainrings and cassettes.

Cleaning and lubricating

Take care not to blast the grease out of the bearings and be sure to replace lubricant where it matters...

The key to proper lubrication is to clean the component before you add any oil. Oiling an already mucky bike will just attract more muck, and cleaning components regularly will keep them running for a long time.

The modern bicycle's chain and gear system is finely tuned. Because the gearbox of a bike is external and therefore open to the elements, it gets a fair amount of abuse. This assists in degrading and corroding all the moving metal parts. Basically, if you leave your bike out in the rain it will rust in a matter of hours, and if you leave the chain, suspension forks and rear shock covered in mud your bike will wear out pretty quickly. Lubrication helps prevent corrosion, but leaving a chain dirty and simply re-lubing it will just help attract more dirt. In the long term, this leads to a build-up of gunge and accelerated chain and sprocket wear.

So, clean your bike and de-grease the chain completely on a regular (two-weekly) basis. Use a water-repellent spray on the rust-sensitive parts and dry them off with a rag. Only use a bicycle-specific lubricant, as some water-repellent sprays and lubricants have solvents in them that can damage the sensitive parts of your bike and ruin your paintwork.

Lubrication

Jockey wheels
Spraying lube all over the jockey wheels just attracts more crud to the chain and rear mech. If you have been riding a lot in wet weather, it's worth stripping the mech and re-greasing the bushes inside the jockey wheels.

Canti studs
Spray a small amount of light dry oil behind the canti (V-brake) and onto the pivot. Obviously, do not spray the rims at the same time! Remove and re-grease the studs on a regular basis as they are steel and will rust if exposed to lots of wet weather.

Cables

Inner cables can be stripped out of the slotted cable guides and lubricated with a Teflon-based lubricant. You can use a heavier lubricant, but these can bung up after a while so use sparingly. If you ride in all weather conditions, or mainly in wet weather, fit a set of cable oilers, which allow you to blast the dirt and water out of the cables and keep them running free. They are very simple to fit and can be installed when you replace the cables.

Chain

Clean the chain and use a dry lube in the summer and a wet lube in the winter or in wet weather. Use a water-repellent spray after washing and lube before every ride.

Rear derailleur (or mech)

Use a thin lube on the rear mech and drop some oil onto the pivots. Work this in by running through the gears a few times. Check the spring inside the mech as it should be clean and rust-free.

Front mech

Like the rear mech, the front mech doesn't need soaking in buckets of heavy lube, but the pivots will benefit from a drop of dry lube squirted and worked into the moving parts. Wipe off any excess with a rag.

Pedals

Clipless pedal mechanisms must be cleaned and lubricated regularly. They will bung up quickly if they are permanently dirty, so clean them if you have been riding (and walking) in mud. Clean the cleats in the shoes too as mud can get impacted into the soles and will prevent the cleats from releasing smoothly.

Brake levers

Like door hinges, brake levers benefit from a squirt of lube every now and again. Make sure that the cable nipple can move freely in the cable-retaining hole. If this goes dry, the friction can damage the lever or break the cable.

Gear levers and Gripshift

It's best not to spray lots of tacky gunge into these sensitive (mainly plastic and nylon) components. A little light oil (dry lube) will keep the water out. Oil the gear levers and Gripshift sparingly and only occasionally.

Suspension forks

Never lubed your forks? Well, you should – a couple of drops of wet lube worked in with a couple of pumps on the bars will keep the seals sweet.

Suspension bikes

As with the forks, the rear suspension unit needs a drop of oil occasionally. The pivots and bushes also need a squirt of lube, especially after wet rides.

Cleaning the chain

1 Chain baths are the best option for cleaning a chain quickly and easily. Take the wheels out of the bike and place the chain on a chain retainer.

2 Clean in between the cassette sprockets and get all of the muck out of the jockey wheels on the derailleur. If you don't, the clean chain will get dirty again as soon as you replace the wheels and turn the pedals.

3 Fill the chain bath with a strong mixture of citrus de-greaser and water.

4 Just hold onto the chain bath and rotate the pedals a few times to get a spotless chain – it's magic!

Troubleshooting

When washing your bike, check it over for dents and cracks and listen to the squeaks and creaks – they can tell you a lot...

Squeaks and creaks

A persistent noise from your bike can drive you mad. Squeaks, ticks and creaks can originate from many different places and they often need a careful process of elimination to find the source of the noise. Noises mean that there is something wrong so take them seriously.

To understand and solve these noises you will need to read through the book, as a properly adjusted bike will be a silent one. However, the main cause of noise from your bike will be dry bearing surfaces or loose components. The friction between surfaces, whether at the threads in your bottom bracket or the clamp on your handlebars, will not be solved by spraying copious amounts of penetrating lubricant into the component – and in particular, don't do this to your handlebars as they could slip and cause a nasty accident. You can't always solve the problem simply by doing the bolts up a little tighter either, as they have recommended tightening torques and may simply need some anti-seize compound applying to

them if they are titanium or aluminium. A persistent rubbing can be something as simple as a cable end hitting the cranks as you pedal, or something less obvious like a broken chain roller, a worn freewheel or a loose hub. All the components should be checked for cracks or splits, and anything that looks unusual should be checked out and replaced if necessary.

So what causes the noises in each component?

Saddle

Very often, the saddle is the cause of pedalling-related noises. As the saddle is usually exposed to the muck off the rear wheel, it gets a lot of abuse and very little cleaning or care. The rails can start to wear out, resulting in a nasty noise as you push on the pedals and move your weight across the saddle. This can be relieved with a spray lube, but the saddle may need replacing. The rails can sometimes get corroded to the seatpost clamp, so check this out too.

How to detect where the noise is coming from

1. Stand on either pedal (you will need to be off the bike to do this) and apply some sideways pressure on the bottom bracket. If it clicks, the cranks

or the bottom bracket may be the root of the noise.

2. Hold the front wheel in your knees and shake the bars from side to side – are the bars tight?

3. Apply the front brake and shake the bike – could the

Aheadset be loose?

4. Grab the saddle with both hands and twist it a little – is it the saddle or the seatpost?

5. Shake the wheels – are the hubs loose?

Seatpost

A dry seatpost will seize up pretty quickly. The residue and corrosion inside the seat tube can make a nasty creaking sound. Remove the seatpost and carefully clean inside the seat tube. Seriously corroded seat tubes will need reaming (cleaning out with a specialist cutting tool). Clean the seatpost with some wire wool and re-apply anti-seize grease before you replace it.

Seatpost clamp

The clamp needs to be a perfect fit and suitably tight. Quick-release seatpost clamps can cause problems if they are not secured tightly enough. If you don't adjust your saddle height as you ride, you could change the quick-release clamp for an Allen key fitting.

Bottom bracket

This is the biggest cause of noise and to solve problems you will have to strip it out and rebuild it regularly.

Cranks

The usual cause of noise is the square taper-type bottom bracket, which can cause all sorts of niggles if assembled incorrectly. Do not grease the taper as it simply forces the cranks on further and damages them. Clean the cranks with disc brake cleaner or a stronger de-greaser and reassemble. Octalink-type bottom brackets need to be cleaned and a small amount of grease used to rebuild them. Always tighten to the correct torque setting and check for tightness regularly.

Chainring bolts

These can often 'dry out' and start to click as a result. Remove them and clean the cranks thoroughly. Then rebuild the chainring bolts using an anti-seize compound.

Chainrings

Worn chainrings cause many more problems than you might think, and very often replacing the chain just makes them worse. Check the teeth for hook-shaped edges and missing teeth. A jumping chain can be dangerous – you'll get thrown forward as you pedal on the down stroke – so keep your chainrings in check.

Chain

This is often the cause of drivetrain noises. Check that the rollers of the chain are all intact and that there is no 'stiff link', which may also cause the chain to jump or skip across the sprockets.

Cassette body

Another cause of drivetrain noises, if the cassette body is old and worn out it will sound terrible. To check this, hold the largest sprocket and rock it from side to side; if there is noticeable play then it may need replacing or tightening. Water and grit can ingress into the freewheel mechanism, which will eventually rust the internals.

Rear mech

Squeaks are usually associated with dry jockey wheel bushings. If the squeak stops when you stop pedalling, it will probably be caused by the pedals, bottom bracket or jockey wheels (the things that rotate as you pedal), which will need lubrication or replacement.

Hubs

If left un-serviced for long periods, the bearings can deteriorate without you knowing it. Loose cones, especially in the rear wheel, can make a racket and will self-destruct pretty quickly – so get them re-adjusted as soon as possible.

Pedals

Worn cleats are a problem for SPD users. Dry threads in the cranks can also cause creaking. This noise will usually occur when 'standing' on the pedals. Remove the pedals and completely de-grease the threads, then apply new grease and re-tighten.

Handlebars

Constant exposure to wet conditions will create problems with the adjustable elements of the bike (anything that clamps two components together). The water gets in and the residue will 'dry out' and provide problems. Handlebars need to be secured in a smooth stem clamp, so check for burrs and clean out regularly.

Stem

Problems with the stem are usually down to the clamp 'drying out'. However, the star-fangled nut or a loose top cap can also creak. As with the handlebars, strip and rebuild and check your Aheadset too.

Aheadset

Dry bearings or broken races will make a very unpleasant creak as you pull on the handlebars. A strip and rebuild will usually eliminate the noise – re-pack the bearings with grease and fresh bearings if you can. Sometimes the crown race on the fork may need re-seating. A knocking sound can mean a loose Aheadset race and may mean the complete unit requires replacement.

Suspension – frame

The frame is usually the cause of noise on suspension bikes. 'Clicking' is a regular fault, and is usually down to dry pivot points or worn DU bushings. Frames with large monocoque frame sections will amplify even the slightest clunk, so it may sound worse than it really is. Spring rear shocks can also rattle loose.

Suspension – fork

Again, any noises are usually down to worn or dried-out bushings. However, be aware of 'hissing' in air forks, as this can mean a leaking seal, or scratching sounds in coil forks, as this can signify a broken spring. Both of these noises will be associated with a loss of performance. Knocking is also a sign of worn bushings, but can also mean that your Aheadset is loose.

Squealing brakes

Most brake noise is down to vibration. Disc brakes will require a regular full clean with a suitable alcohol-based rotor cleaner, and regular replacing of the pads. Check that all the calliper bolts are tight and that the rotor is secured correctly to the hub.

Other problems

Ticking

This usually happens when you pedal and could be caused by:

- the cable hitting the crank/your feet as you pedal
- a loose cassette sprocket
- pedal spindles
- the front mech hitting the inside of the right hand crank – you will need to re-adjust it

Rubbing or whirring from disc brakes

- Whirring usually means that the pads are worn too low
- Check that the wheels are in straight
- Re-centre the brakes
- Check whether the rotor is buckled or damaged

Chain 'skipping'

- Check the indexing – it should run straight on the sprocket
- If you have crashed recently, the mech hanger may well have been bent

THE MOST COMPREHENSIVE RANGE OF QUALITY BIKE TOOLS
ON THE PLANET. PARK TOOL IS USED BY MORE PRO MECHANICS
THAN ANY OTHER TOOL BRAND, PROUDLY SPONSORING TEAM SKY,
BMC RACING AND GARMIN BARRACUDA.

ParkTool®

www.parktool.com

DISTRIBUTED IN THE UK & IRELAND BY
MADISON·CO·UK

Contact Points

Handlebars, grips, bar ends and seatposts

Whirling your legs around while perched on a utility seat powering a thoroughbred speed machine is never going to be as comfortable as, say, watching a favourite old movie in your electric recliner before an open fire. However, while it may make you a little sore at first, riding a bike should not hurt. If it does, something's wrong and, assuming you have been sold a bike that fits you, it usually has to do with the contact points – the saddle, bars and pedals and the way they interact.

The wrong saddle is going to be hard on the backside and genitals, particularly, although not exclusively, for women. There is no need for that, the bicycle industry has specially adapted shorter wider saddles designed to solve the problem for all types of female anatomy, and sort the pressure problems for men too. Similarly painful pressure on legs, lower back, shoulders and neck are caused by a faulty relationship between saddle, pedals and bars and can be adjusted out.

"The saddle, bars and pedals are the parts you will want to adjust first"

Assuming the bike fits...

Any bike should fit the rider. A dedicated race machine should fit precisely, which is why specialist bike fitting services are becoming more common in the road bike business. But while less precise machines, utility bikes and general mountain bikes give greater latitude, there is still only so much you can do altering saddle height and bar width.

Finding the right riding position

The wrong riding position can cause you all sorts of problems, in particular back pain. Here are some suggestions to help you get it right. A knowledgable person overseeing the process, or failing that photographs or a full length mirror, can help you as you adjust the contact points to achieve the best balanced position

Saddle height

Too low

Riding for prolonged periods with a low saddle will place excessive strain on the knees. You will see downhill mountain bikers and trials riders with their saddles low to keep them out of the way on rough terrain but don't copy them. It's OK for short periods of pedalling only.

Too high

This often creates back problems as the rider will have to stretch to reach the pedals at the bottom of each stroke, which tilts the pelvis and pulls on the lower back muscles. The same principle applies if you bob back and forth excessively when riding hard as your back will tire and start to hurt. This is often why back pain is especially bad after a hard hilly ride or race.

About right

The knee should be slightly bent at the bottom of the pedal stroke. An easy way to judge this is to have the heel of your foot on the pedal with your leg fully

extended at the bottom of the stroke, then pedal backwards. If you find that you rock from side to side excessively, your saddle is too high and you need to reset it so you feel smooth in this position. This way, when the ball of your foot is placed on the pedal there will be a bit of extra slack built in to your saddle height.

N.B. This is only a guide – some riders will require more careful adjustments. If you alter your saddle height, do it by small increments of no more than 5 mm at a time and give yourself a few weeks to get used to it. That's why it's best to change position during the winter months as you won't be riding as regularly.

Stem fore/aft position

Too cramped

This will make you arch your back and stress the lower muscles. It also means you ride with your weight further forward, which will make the steering sluggish.

Too stretched

This usually forces you to lock out your arms and strain your neck to see ahead, both of which will contribute towards low back pain. The handling will feel sketchy and a bit too light.

About right

A balanced position means that you will be able to stretch out comfortably and bend your arms to assist in shock absorption. With the stem the right length,

Tools required:

. Torque Wrench
. set of Allen keys

UPGRADE...
Hydration Packs
Fitting bottle cages to certain styles of MTB can be tricky, so a great alternative is to invest in a hydration backpack.

your weight will be better distributed over the bike – if it is too short, the saddle will have to be pushed too far back; too long and the saddle will be too far forward.

Saddle fore/aft position

Too far back

This is good for climbing power and pedalling comfort over a long ride, but places extra strain on neck, arm and shoulder muscles.

Too far forward

You'll get a lot of pedal power in this position, but it places a lot of stress on the larger muscles and can cause fatigue and tightness in the upper leg.

About right

You should be able to pass a vertical line (use a bit of string and a weight for a plumb line) through the centre of your knee (the bony lump just behind your knee cap) and the pedal spindle when the cranks are parallel to the ground.

FAQ: *Is full suspension a benefit on a general mountain bike?*

The ups and downs of the trail are always going to place excessive strain on your body – in short, you have to put up with the battering that your bike does, but your bike's built to take it and you're not. Suspension can work wonders for some people's problems as it can often reduce the bashes, but it does also mean extra work (in the case of full suspension) on the climbs. This can lead to fatigue-induced back pain. Suspension shock posts are a good idea if you can't afford a new bike and if your back ache is worse after a really rough ride. Always remember to use your arms and knees to help absorb the big hits on the descents and try to remain relaxed and comfortable on the climbs.

First adjustments

Get your flat bar bike home and these are the first things you'll change

Brake lever angle

 Inexperienced riders tend to place the levers flat to the handlebars, but the angle of the brake lever should be similar to the angle your arm takes to reach the handlebar; your wrists should be as straight and comfortable as possible when they are placed on the bars. This enables the tendons and muscles in your arm to pull in a linear motion, which is the most efficient way.

 Adjusting the lever angle is simple. There is a 4 or 5 mm Allen bolt under the brake-lever clamp and, depending on the make of your bike, this can be accessed easily. The brake lever can also be swapped if you prefer the left to be the rear brake, for example. The lever can also be moved inwards or outwards on the bar. Get one lever spot-on before you start on the other one to give you a reference point for how the lever was previously set.

 The gear pod adjusting bolt is also here. You may have to depress the levers to get the Allen key into the socket. Bondhus Allen keys, which can be used at an angle, are a good idea for reaching awkward fixing bolts like these. The pods are designed to fit snugly to the brake lever, but be aware that the cable adjuster needs to be accessed easily – so don't rest it where you can't reach it.

Brake lever reach

 Setting the lever reach is quite simple, but you do need to assess where your fingers will pull on the lever. Ideally, your first two fingers should be able to fold easily over the lever. As the lever is activated, the fingers shouldn't feel any strain as they pull the lever towards the bar. This may sound obvious now, but if your fingers cramp up on a long descent you're in trouble.

 All cable-activated brake levers have a reach adjustment screw. So, if you have small hands, or want to get more purchase on the lever, look to experiment with it. Screwing this lever in will also affect the cable length, so double check the brakes before you ride off. If you adjust it a great deal, be aware that the lever may hit the handlebars before the brakes activate. Experiment with cable adjustment too, as this can give the brake more 'feel' at the lever.

 Hydraulic disc brakes also have a reach adjustment screw. Depending on which system you are using, it is usually behind the lever on the plunger spigot. Only make small adjustments as this can affect the pull of the lever.

Seatpost and saddle

 4 In the 'full-on' braking position the fingers should close over the brake and lock the wheels up. Once you are happy that this is the case, check that the levers are symmetrical and tighten all the fixing bolts.

The brake and gear levers need to be tight enough that they don't move under braking or shifting, but not so tight that they cannot move in the event of a crash.

 1 The seatpost should be greased regularly, unless it is made out of carbon fibre. Mountain Bikers will want to lower the seatpost out on the trail for long rocky descents and technical sections, which means you will need to be able to move the saddle quickly. A seatpost can seize very quickly if you neglect to re-grease it regularly.

FAQ: *Do women need special bikes to fit them?*

Women's bikes are designed specifically to suit the female physique. In general terms, women tend to have a shorter body and longer legs, proportionally, than men. This means that a long top tube will have to be countered with an upright seatpost without any layback and a shorter stem. It is even better to have a shorter top tube too, which is why there are so many brands that have a specific women's bike in their range. Women's saddles are wider to offer more support, and handlebars may be less wide to accommodate narrower shoulders.

 2 The saddle should be flat (line it up with a brick wall or use a spirit level to check this). If you feel the saddle needs to point downward, it is probably too high in relation to the handlebars.

 3 Check that the seatpost quick release is tight in the frame, as it is possible for this to slip gradually over a long ride. The principle of this lever is the same as that of a wheel quick release. If you have trouble securing the seatpost (and you find you don't change your saddle height very often), change the collar for one that fastens with an Allen bolt as these can be more secure.

CHANGE & UPGRADE
Road seatposts

Two components which a keen rider can upgrade to save weight and increase stiffness...

The shaft of an aluminium seatpost should always be smeared with anti-seize grease before inserting it into the seat tube. It should slide in without any pressure being applied and there shouldn't be any side-to-side movement before the clamp bolt is tightened. The anti-seize grease will also prevent the different materials from seizing together. When setting your saddle height, never go beyond the minimum insert mark usually etched into the post (see 'Length', below). If you have to, the chances are that the post is too short or your bike is too small!

The saddle clamp is in two halves – one holds the saddle to the post and the other adjusts the angle of the saddle.

Length

Seatposts (or seat pins) come in several lengths, with 250mm and 300mm being the most common in road bikes. As I've said, you need a pin that leaves plenty of material in the frame – pins usually have a line to indicate the minimum insertion level ('Min. Insertion') or maximum height ('Max. Ht.'). Don't exceed this – it not only protects the seatpost, but also prevents

placing excess strain on the top of the frame's seat tube/clamp area, which can easily be distorted by the extra leverage on the little bit left in the frame.

Size (diameter)

This depends on the material that the frame is made of. Steel and standard aluminium frames usually come in 26.4–27.2mm sizes, but some specialist frames can be as little as 25mm and as much as 32.7mm. Getting the recommended size for

your frame is essential, as even 0.2mm either way can make a difference to the correct fit. If it's too big, it can swell the seat tube and make it difficult to fit or remove – if it's too small, it can move about, damaging the collar and distorting the top of the seat tube.

Fitting saddles

There are several types of seatpost cradle and most good quality posts have one bolt-fixing. This means that the cradle will be removable and easy to rebuild. Saddles now have cut-away sides and this makes it much easier to access under the rails and fit the top cradle.

1 To adjust the saddle angle, loosen the post at the back bolt. Then the front bolt can either be tightened to point the nose of the saddle downwards, or loosened to point the nose up.

4 Clean the insides of the clamp. Dry off and wipe with a light oil. Don't use grease on the saddle clamping area.

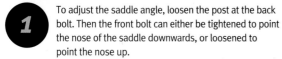

2 Use a Bondhus round-headed Allen key to access the bolt to the rear of the post – this prevents scratching the post and allows a full rotation of the bolt.

5 Single-clamp seatpost bolts need lubricating around the wedges and spacers – again, use a light oil.

3 Clean and thoroughly de-grease any seatpost clamp serrations. Here, the black oxide indicates an area of friction where the cradle has been worked loose and started to wear.

6 Be sure to clean off excess lube here – the seatpost is in direct line of the rear wheel which directs road grime onto the clamp area.

 **EDITOR'S TIP**

"I prefer seatposts with duel bolts, they are harder to adjust but stay put and don't rattle loose"

Noises

The seatpost can be a source of annoying creaks and squeaks. Usually, a thorough clean and rebuild of the clamp will eradicate the creaks. Remember to check the saddle rails too, especially where they join the underside of the saddle. A squirt of lube into the ends of the rails can be enough to keep friction at bay.

7 Remove and clean carbonfibre posts regularly. Use a bike polish that can buff the post to a shine.

8 Clean the inside of the seat tube. Don't grease carbon posts – if the frame is tight-fitting or in poor internal condition, you may well be better off with aluminium. If you must fit carbon, seat tubes can be reamed out to clean up the insides.

9 Make sure there are no sharp edges and burrs inside the seat tube, and that the seatpost collar is undone, before trying to insert the carbon post. Scratches in the surface of the lacquer (like these shown here) are OK as long as they're below the insertion point – deep scratches and gouges are not OK. Any damage to the surface layer of carbon means that the post should be replaced immediately.

10 If you're using a carbon post, fit a saddle collar like this Campagnolo one. This prevents the collar from binding up around the back of the seat tube slot and damaging the post. If you have a standard seat collar, you can turn the collar around so that the slots are opposite one another. Damage in this area can be catastrophic, so be careful.

11 Only tighten to manufacturers' recommended torque settings. If your post still slips, don't keep tightening it – the chances are that you need a different-diameter post or your frame need attention. Over-tightening carbon posts can crush the post's tube, so be careful. If you have to tighten up harder, change for an aluminium or titanium post.

CHANGE & UPGRADE
Saddles

While it's highly likely your bike came with a saddle included, you may feel the time's right for an upgrade, and knowing your options is key for a comfortable ride...

Are you sitting comfortably? Changing a saddle is one of the more popular upgrades going, but ensuring you buy a seat suited to the job is absolutely crucial. Anything not fit for purpose could make you're cycling experience a miserable one.

Road Saddles

Road saddles don't tend to have lots of padding, it's an area which can easily add weight to a bike, but that's not to say they're uncomfortable. Road cyclists tend to wear shorts with a chamois in the gusset, which goes further than you'd think to improve comfort, but sitting steadily astride a rigid race bike in comfort depends on the rider's sit bones. As a result a try-before-you-buy purchasing philosophy is a good one.

A light, comfortable saddle is best suited to svelte racing bikes. The profile of this particular saddle is very flat, which enables a rider to shift around easily to obtain greater power and comfort.

EDITOR'S TIP

"Shift your body onto the tip of the saddle to generate more power on the flat, and toward the rear to pedal more affectively when climbing"

Sitting pretty?
Being comfortable encourages more time on the bike but a new saddle can improve looks and also save excess weight.

Mountain Bike Saddles

Mountain bike saddles have a need for great cushioning to absorb the jarring terrain; they also need to be durable in the event of a crash. Most brands take this into careful consideration and feature hard wearing covers and reinforced hulls on their off-road models, ensuring a happy marriage of comfort and safety.

Like other areas of a mountain bike anatomy, saddle design is often partnered to particular style of riding. This is a good example of an all-rounder, it's lightweight but durable design is suitable for most types of riding.

UPGRADE...
Cables and Housing
Replace gear and brake cables regularly to keep components healthy; consider waterproof housing to increase the time between services.

Women's Saddles

Women need to pay greater attention to their saddle choice than men as their sit bones vary more significantly in size and shape. Unfortunately, men currently have a far greater selection of saddles to choose from than women, but many manufactures have demo saddles available and will supply shops with their complete ranges to try before purchase.

Offering more padding, a specific women's saddle is highly advised. They're anatomically adapted to fit better, with a wider rear offering more support and comfort to female cyclists.

CHANGE & UPGRADE
Road handlebar set-up
The correct handlebar choice plays a huge part in getting comfortable on the bike

Position

There's a simple test for checking your handlebar position – take a look at your handlebar tape. Where is it most worn? On the tops? Behind the brake levers? Or on the drops? Many riders hardly ever use the drop part of their bars, usually because they're too low and too far away to be used comfortably. Handlebar choice can play a great part in getting comfortable, so select the bar that has the right reach, width and drop, as riders generally use bars that are too big in all these dimensions.

Bar measurement

Most manufacturers state the bar's measurement from centre to centre. Standard road bars are 42cm, and these will be fine for almost everyone, but some women and younger riders may opt for smaller bars with less reach. Bars are available in 38cm to 48cm sizes, and some companies offer other designs that are even wider. It's best to buy handlebars at the width of your shoulders. The wider the bar, the more control you'll have over the steering, hence cyclo-cross riders often go a size up – they can get more leverage out of a wider bar. But a wider bar takes more effort, as your arms are best used parallel, so narrow bars are more efficient for sprinting and climbing.

Round bars

Once upon a time, all bars were round. Thankfully, there are a few companies that still make round handlebars. They usually come in shallow- and deep-drop form. The former are better for riders with smaller hands, and the latter for sprinters and track riders.

Ergo bars

Most bar manufacturers offer a variety of handlebar shapes. These are intended to offer more comfortable hand positions and ergonomic comfort than round bars – however, if set up incorrectly they can provide the exact opposite. Generally, Ergo bars offer a flatter section just behind the brake levers, intended for sprinting and descending in comfort. Set this angle to suit you before you worry about how the levers fit. My advice is to buy (cheaper) aluminium bars and try several makes until you know exactly what suits you.

1 When installing handlebars, take care not to scratch the surface of the bar. Scratches act as stress raisers and may lead to failure over time.

2 There's usually a mark or series of marks on the bar where the centre section is. This will also give you an idea of the preferred angle of the bar. Line this up with the front cap of the stem.

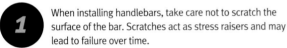

3 The flat ends of the bar should be at the bottom of the bend, either parallel with the stem or the floor. Round bars usually need the flat part pointing towards the axle of the rear hub. When fitting new bars, establish the right riding angles, and that the drop position is feeling natural and comfortable, before you start to add the brake levers.

4 To fit the levers, first remove the clip from the rear of the lever – don't try to push the lever on with the clip still attached, as it'll only scratch the surface of the bar (especially important with carbon bars).

5 Slide the clip into position – they're a snug fit so should hold their position OK. Some bars have a rough section behind the bar at the lever position to add grip and indicate the point to position the lever.

6 All makes of lever (pictured is Shimano) have a recessed 5mm Allen nut inside the lever housing, which attaches to the bolt trapped in the lever clip. It helps to pull the rubber hood back a little to locate the lever housing over the bolt.

Creaking bars?

Most noises from handlebars can easily be eliminated by stripping the bar from the stem, cleaning it with parts cleaner and rebuilding the stem with fresh grease or copper slip on the fixing bolts. Take the stem off, check the fork steerer and clean it too.

EDITOR'S TIP

"Replace bars after bad crashes and after a couple of years' heavy use. Failure is rare but if it happens you won't get much warning"

7 On Shimano this can be accessed via a channel on the outside of the lever hood.

8 SRAM and Campagnolo levers require the lever hood to be rolled forwards (be careful not to rip the hood as you pull it over the thumb lever on Campagnolo levers). Use a T-bar Allen key to access the nut on these types.

9 Line the tip of the brake lever up with the base of the bar (flat section) – use a ruler and get this approximate before trying different hand positions to get the feel right.

10 The controls can be positioned parallel to the ground – use a ruler to line them up with the flat top section of the bar. Don't over-tighten them, as the levers' clips can easily break. Levers can also bend if they're not allowed to move a little in the event of a crash.

CHANGE & UPGRADE
Road control lever set-up

The correct riding position is with the hands placed naturally on the lever hoods

Lever position can take a while to get spot-on – many riders are always tweaking their bars and lever position. The 'correct' riding position is with the hands placed naturally on the lever hoods – if you find them too hard to reach, it may be that the levers need moving towards you or that the stem is too long, or even that the bike is too long.

With the hands wrapped around the lever hoods it's easy to change gear and brake without too much effort. If you have to remove your hands from the tops of the bars and move them forwards to brake or shift, there's something wrong with your bar and lever set-up. It shouldn't require you to move much at all, and above all it should be comfortable.

It's essential that you can comfortably reach the brake levers, wrapping your fingers around the lever to get full leverage. Ergo bars don't always allow this, especially for riders with smaller hands.

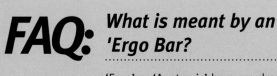

FAQ: *What is meant by an 'Ergo Bar?*

'Ergo' or 'Anatomic' bars are drop handlebars with one, sometimes more, flat spots (straight sections) which some riders find to be more comfortable for their hands.

CHANGE & UPGRADE
Road pedals and cleat set-up

Clipless pedals offer the most efficient power transfer because they let you pull as well as push

Pedals

Most road cyclists now use clipless pedals, and toe clips have become a thing of the past. The system was introduced in 1985 by Look, a ski company, which used a cleat screwed to the sole of the shoe which snaps into a sprung fastening on the pedal as with skis. They release with a twist of the foot. While being fixed to the bike in this way takes a little getting used to, clipless pedals offer the most efficient power transfer because they let you pull up on the pedals as well as push down. There are many types available today, the most popular being those from Look, Time, Speedplay and Shimano.

1 Before you start, remember that pedals have a left- and right-handed thread. Most systems stamp 'L' and 'R' on the axle somewhere so you know which is which. On Shimano pedals, this is stamped on the flat part of the pedal spindle, where the spanner attaches.

3 Left- and right-hand pedal threads tighten up in the direction of pedalling. The easiest way to remember this is to hold the pedal up to the crank, flat on your fingers, and spin the cranks backwards as if you were freewheeling.

2 Pedal threads must be greased. Use a good-quality, waterproof synthetic or anti-seize grease. Clean the threads and re-grease them regularly. Because axles are made out of steel and cranks are made out of aluminium, there can be problems with threads seizing. Also, be careful not to cross-thread the cranks, as they can easily be ruined.

4 Some pedals have Allen-key fittings, and these usually require a long Allen key to either tighten correctly or, more importantly, provide enough leverage to remove.

5 Tighten the pedals to the manufacturer's recommended torque setting. Hold the opposite crank or the rear wheel and use the added leverage to help you tighten the pedals.

6 To remove the pedals, it's probably easiest if you stand the bike on the floor. You'll remove the pedal in the direction of the freewheel, so you may have to hold the opposite crank to prevent it from spinning.

7 If you're using clipless pedals for the first time (and they have tension adjustment), back the springs right off so that the release tension is minimal. This helps getting used to the system and enables you to get out easily to put your foot down. Over the first few days you can tighten them.

8 As Speedplay pedals are double-sided, they're a lot easier for first-time users – there's no need to 'flip the pedals' to step into them. The cleats are the spring-and-release system.

"The cleat will wear more quickly on the side you release most often when you stop, so swap cleats around for longer life"

Pedal cleats

Once you've installed the pedals, you can fit the cleats to your shoes. Most shoes adopt the three-bolted system, which makes it easiest to set the angle of cleat and retain a solid fixing for the step-out flick. Make sure that the bolts are the right length and don't protrude into the sole. Look to align your feet

in the way you walk. Foot alignment is becoming a very serious business and most good bike-fitters will now recommend that you see a podiatrist to get custom-made footbeds, which provide stability and align your feet for more efficient pedalling. The pedal axle needs to be directly under the ball of your foot, so spend

time and get it right. Regular cleaning and lubrication are essential. Always pick out any of the jammed-in mud and grit from around the cleat, as it can prevent stepping out of the binding. Walking in road-shoe plates wears the cleats out quickly and is pretty dangerous anyway. Rubber covers are available for most pedal systems, and they'll prevent slipping on hard floors and avoid wear to the cleat. Worn cleats are likely to release easily and when you least expect them to (in a sprint!).

1   Assess the position of the ball of your foot over the pedal axle. Mark on the side of your shoe where the ball of your foot is, then mark a line across the sole of your shoe. This is where the cleat will be placed. Use this reference to decide which set of holes in the plates to use.

2   Prepare the threads in the plates with copper slip. The cleats will rust pretty quickly if you don't. You can replace these screws with stainless-steel bolts (you can buy these from an engineering supplier), as they're less likely to rust up and will therefore last longer.

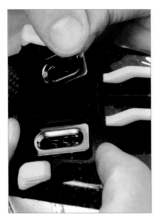

3 Most systems have slotted washers to allow plenty of fore and aft adjustments. A light grease on these will help keep them easy to adjust.

4 Tighten the shoe cleats to the recommended torque setting. Don't over-tighten them, as the threads can strip very easily, in which case you would have to replace the sole insert. Check the bolts regularly, as they can shake loose.

5 The correct cleat position is with the ball or pushing part of your foot over the pedal axle. This requires measuring and some trial and error to get spot-on.

6 Speedplay cleats have a four-bolt fitting cleat and they're supplied with a plate that fixes to the three-bolt-pattern shoe. The cleats are also the sprung part of the system and need regular cleaning and lubricating (use a very lightweight oil). The cleat bolts should be Loctited into place, as they cannot be too tight. Over-tightening the bolts will prevent the springs from moving and therefore prevent the float.

7 Time pedals now have the same three-bolt pattern cleat fitting as Look and other manufacturers. The brass cleat snaps into the pedal-binding and needs to be kept clean.

KNOW HOW

Noises

Noisy or creaking pedals can be caused by worn cleats or simply dry threads. Re-grease the threads regularly and replace your cleats before they start releasing on their own.

CHANGE & UPGRADE
Mountain bike handlebars

Mountain bike bars raise the rider higher at the front of the bike for added control

Handlebars

It is best to buy handlebars at the length you are going to use them, but some bikes come with a very wide set that you may want to cut down a little. The wider the bar, the more control you will have over the steering, but with very wide bars you may find you get stuck (literally) in the tighter sections of single track. Cross-country racers may also prefer a narrower bar for comfort on longer distances. It is not recommended that you cut down carbon bars, so buy the correct length. Always measure them up to a set you are used to.

Tools required:
- hairspray
- an old spoke
- Stanley knife
- pair of pincers
- zip ties
- Griptite or touch-up paint

1 Take care when installing handlebars not to twist them in the stem too much or otherwise scratch the surface of the bar. Scratches create a stress riser and can lead to failure at a later date. There is usually a mark on the bar where the centre section is. This will also give you an idea of the preferred angle of the sweep.

2 Centre the bars in the stem. The controls can then be positioned at equal distances from the stem. Measure the position of the gear and brake shifters and set them to the correct torque setting. Do not over-tighten them, as the levers are sensitive and could bend if they are not allowed to 'move' a little in the event of a crash.

3 The main advantage of riser bars over flat bars is that they place the rider higher at the front of the bike, thus giving a more 'controlled' position. Risers should be positioned so that the sweep faces towards the rider. Some downhill racers prefer higher and wider riser bars, as they give added control.

Fitting bar ends
When fitting bar ends make sure you get them at a comfortable riding angle – usually between 5 and 15 degrees. The best way is to line them up with the angle of your stem.

Cutting out grip ends

To cut out the end of a grip for fitting bar ends, slide onto an old bar and tap with a mallet. Like coring apples...

Grips and bar-ends

1 Removing your old grips is really easy. If you don't need them again, just cut them off with a Stanley knife. Alternatively, use an old spoke to pull the grip away from the bar then squirt some spray lube up the inside (this may need working around a bit if the grip is well stuck on). Wrap some tape around the threaded bit of the spoke to stop it scratching the bars. If you are going to reuse the grip, don't use spray lube as it will only make them spin when you re-fit them. Use some hairspray instead.

2 If you are fitting a grip shifter or a bar end, you'll need to cut down the grip a bit. Measure it carefully next to the old grip or against the bar. Cut away the extra part carefully with a Stanley knife. You can tidy up the ragged end with a pair of pincers. If you are using Gripshift, place the un-cut end next to the shifter. This will give you a flush fitting for better shifting.

3 Use some hairspray to fit the grips. This will allow you to push the grip on very easily, and it also sets like a lacquer and seals the grip to the bar. It's not sticky though, so it won't make a mess of your bars and so on. Some riders use car spraypaint as it seals out the water and prevents your grips from spinning, but it can be a bit messy.

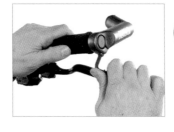

4 If you are fitting bar ends, make sure you don't over-tighten them; they only need to be tight enough so you don't move them with riding force. It's best to let them move a bit to protect your bike in the event of a crash – if they are too tight then you risk twisting the bar as well as damaging the bar end. Always put a plug in the end of the bar – crashing with open-ended bars is dangerous even if they have bar ends on them, and plugs will also stop water and mud getting into your bars.

5 Bar-end stops prevent the grip from pulling off under pressure. Locking grips are even better as they do not rotate at all. Also fit bash ends if you're into jumping or crash a lot, as they will absorb the shock and prevent the ends of the bar being damaged. A good tip is to zip-tie the grip tightly to the bar. Most grips have a slot cut into them for the bar to bed into. Use a small tie for the best results and place the knuckle bit underneath so you don't catch your hands on it. Fuse wire can work just as well, but make sure you tuck it away so you don't catch your gloves or hands on the ends. Wrap the wire around the grip a couple of times before twisting the two ends tightly together.

CHANGE & UPGRADE
Mountain bike pedals & seatposts

While being generally more robust, mountain and utility bike pedals and seatposts can be treated for the most part like the road versions

Of course mountain bike pedals get the most abuse. They are invariably the first things to hit the ground in a crash and, as they stick out from the bike at the bottom of your pedal stroke, they bash stuff like rocks as you hammer through the singletrack.

While most cross-country MTB riders tend to favour clipless pedals (often Shimano's SPD type), a big platform version is popular in the dirt and flat pedals are very common amongst all-mountain riders, who need to get their feet down on extreme terrain, as well as with dirt jumpers and trials riders. Flat pedals are reassuringly robust and make it far easier to jump ship in (or preferably just before) a crash. The advent of sticky rubber soled boots (a development of climbing technology) which stick to the pedals and prevent the foot jerking loose on rough ground has made flats more usable, to the extent that a world class contender like Australian rider Sam Hill prefers to use them on extreme downhill tracks.

Tools required:
- waterproof synthetic or anti-seize grease
- torque wrench
- Allen key
- lubricant
- pedal collar tool
- vice
- grease
- spanners

Care of the SPD pedal

The Shimano Pedalling Dynamics system was invented as the first MTB-specific clipless pedal and has remained a firm favourite...

1 If you are using SPD pedals for the first time, back the springs off so that the release tension is minimal. As the pedal is double-sided and has a spring for each side, make sure you loosen the bolts on either side of the pedal.

2 Regular cleaning and lubrication is essential. Rebuild the bearings regularly, but replace the bearings every time you service the pedals to keep them rolling for longer.

3 Binding and loose bearings are usually the tell-tale signs of a bent axle. Most Shimano pedals use the same cartridge-style axle, which can be replaced. There is a special tool to undo the collars on the pedals. Place this in a vice for ease of use.

4 Place the special collar tool in a vice and loosen the pedal (there is an arrow on the pedal collar to show you which direction to turn it). The pedal body can be removed and cleaned thoroughly with de-greaser and a toothbrush.

5 With the axle removed, you can assess the damage. Hold the bearing part and spin the axle stub. If it is wobbly and the bearings are very loose, you will probably have to replace the complete assembly.

6 Remove the lock nut and the top cone. If the bearings are dull and pitted and the cones have similar pitting and marks, you will be better off replacing the complete unit. You can adjust the cones with this special tool or with the appropriate sized spanners. Readjusting the cones is very similar to adjusting wheel bearings. You are looking to set the collar so it has no play and isn't binding onto the bearings.

7 Before replacing a new axle or the restored old one, pack the pedal body with grease.

8 Finally, tighten the pedal body onto the axle using the same tool. You only need to tighten it by hand – over-tightening can break the collar and bind the bearings.

A mountain bike classic

The SPD pedal is another significant Shimano 'invention'. Shimano took the clipless cleat idea from the road pedals of the late eighties and made it into a system that you can walk in, as well as cycle. Now used by millions of mountain bikers, this has to be one of the most useful mountain bike inventions. Efficient pedalling and a mud-clearing design make for a very user-friendly system.

The MTB seatpost

Your mountain bike has a smaller frame than your road bike; it's stronger and makes it easier to get your feet down when everything goes wrong on rough terrain. Radical terrain

is normally ridden standing on the pedals for a lower centre of gravity and better use of body weight, so the seatpost is often lowered out of the way when the going gets very tough. Because the frames are smaller, the seatposts are mostly longer with all the extra leverage that means, so you will find more steel used for strength than carbon fibre for lightness. Otherwise MTB posts are similar to the road version, only needing to be well greased so they can easily be slid out of the way, either using the quick release or one of the special systems that are becoming more popular as improved suspension opens up the wildest mountain terrain to the modern MTB.

The Drivetrain

Where raw power becomes controlled speed

A toothed chain ring, powered by cranks and driving, via a linked chain, a smaller sprocket, which turns the wheel, is Victorian engineering. And it's so effective that even today it remains the favoured system on the most demanding applications today and you will find little real difference between mountain and road bikes in this department.

The bit that used not to work so well was the crank axle. Cranks are long levers which, when pushed by the biggest muscles in the human body, transfer huge force into the axle that supports the chainrings and the bearing it works in, which goes by the confusing name of the bottom bracket and runs in the lowest point on the bike frame, the bottom bracket shell. Until recently these were Victorian engineering too, loose ball bearings running in a cup and cone structure between the main components and sheer hell to adjust properly. Now largely

"The confidence to replace a bottom bracket shows you are becoming a serious mechanic..."

replaced by cartridge bearings fitting inside the bottom bracket shell, these too are being replaced by oversize bearing outside the shell, which allow oversized axles to deal with the forces

The road drivetrain

The powerhouse of the bicycle, the drivetrain takes a real beating and needs all the care and attention you have time to give it...

Chainsets, cranks and chainrings

Chainrings and cranks combine to form the chainset, and these are the engine room of the bike – that is, the bit that gets all the power directly from your legs and helps you rip up the road. There are now several systems available, and most manufacturers have a solution for the chainset and bottom bracket (BB) unit. Compatibility is always the main issue. For example, Campagnolo square-taper won't work with Shimano square-taper BB axles and vice versa. ISIS drive was developed by a group of smaller manufacturers who kept to the same design for inter-compatibility. External bearing cups are now the future, and most big manufacturers are making a system like this.

Tools:

- Allen keys
- crank puller and spanner
- torque wrench and 8mm Allen socket
- copper slip
- chainline tool
- lock-ring tools
- vice or large spanner

Main BB/chainset types:

- JIS Square Taper (Japanese Industry Standard) – Shimano and Far-Eastern manufacturers standard square taper BB fitting
- Campagnolo Square Taper – as used by Campagnolo up until 2007
- Octalink – Shimano's step away from the square taper; used a bigger BB axle and a machined keyway fitting
- ISIS Drive – the International Splined Interface Standard (all manufacturers except Campagnolo and Shimano)
- External Bearing – Shimano's Hollowtech II and Truvativ (SRAM)
- Ultra-Torque – Campagnolo's take on the external bearing BB and crank system

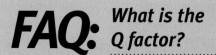

FAQ: **What is the Q factor?**

It's the distance across the pedal faces, which dictates how far apart your legs are on the bike. Usually around 145mm for road bikes.

UPGRADE...
Cassettes

Cassettes are integral to a bike's anatomy, better materials such as titanium prolong lifespan, aide shifting and are noticeably lighter.

Care and maintenance

Removing cranks. The first step to changing and upgrading your drivetrain

Removing cranks is simple, as long as you use the right tools. Replacing cartridge BBs couldn't be easier, so if you're still running a cup and loose ball-bearing bracket, you should think about changing soon. A lot of BBs are 'fit-and-forget' units, i.e. once it's in, you don't need to worry about it.

The crank puller

The crank puller should be inserted well into the crank thread and be sure to tighten it carefully. It's a powerful tool. Pulling just a few threads or cross threading it can strip the crank thread and your crank is scrap.

1 On standard cranks, the fixing bolt has an 8mm Allen head with the washer as an integral part of the bolt. Old-style cranks still use a 14mm or 15mm hex-headed bolt and washer that can be protected by a separate dust cap.

2 The bolt has a washer/cover around it to protect the threads inside the crank. There may also be a washer (usually on Campagnolo only) behind the bolt, so make sure that you remove this.

3 Once you've removed the bolts and washers, remove the crank using a crank puller. This tool is essential for taking the cranks off the bike, and good ones won't damage the threads or the end of the axle. Clean out any dirt from the crank threads with a squirt of spray lube.

4 The crank puller has a central bolt, and once it's threaded into the crank as far as it'll go, the central bolt can be tightened to 'push' the crank away from the BB axle. Undo the centre bolt first so it fits as flush as possible, being careful to get it in straight.

5 The easiest puller to use is one with an arm attached to the end of the centre bolt – they are useful for travelling toolkits when you might not have room for a big spanner. However, it's worth noting that most pullers accept a 15mm spanner, so you can use a pedal-spanner to tighten the removing bolt.

6 ISIS and Octalink cranks have a hollow round axle and therefore require a larger head on the crank puller – Park's remover can accept either types and is supplied with a pair of different-sized adaptors. ISIS axles have a symmetrical splined pattern on the axle. Shimano Octalink cranks are very different, so don't try to mix them up.

7 Once you've correctly inserted the puller, tighten the arm (or central bolt) towards the BB axle. The arm rests on the end of the axle and the pushing/pulling motion forces the crank off the square-axle taper. The crank will try to drop off onto the floor, so be careful to keep hold of it.

8 Some cranks have 'captive' bolts. These have a puller built in, and the crank bolt is held captive so that the undoing action of the crank bolt also removes the crank for you. These are recommended on ISIS and Octalink, and are also fitted to some Shimano cranksets.

9 Removing captive-bolted cranks just requires one 8mm Allen key. They're a great idea for touring bikes and commuters.

10 Always retighten cranks to the recommended torque setting and check them after the first ride – they can loosen off slightly.

Chainring bolts
Chainring bolts should be tightened gradually and in sequence (that is, not from left to right but from opposite bolt to opposite bolt). It's the same principle as bolting on a car wheel.

CHANGE & UPGRADE
Chainrings
How to replace worn rings or change your ratios

Chainrings

Fitting chainrings is very simple, but make sure that you get the correct size for your crank. Chainrings come in hundreds of sizes and are made in a variety of manufacturing processes – stamped, CNC-machined and sometimes part-cut/part-machined. The current trend is for ramps and rivets to assist the chain in shifting. The usual drive set-up will be 53-/39-toothed rings, but any number of combinations are possible on most cranks.

Chainring bolts

Chainring bolts are made from steel, titanium or aluminium. Steel bolts are probably the best, as they're cheap and strong. They need greasing every now and then, as they can seize if left to rust. Use copper grease on the bolts. Titanium bolts are very light but very expensive, and also require special attention if left for long periods of time, as they can seize up. Aluminium bolts are really light but not very strong, and can snap off. Use plenty of copper slip or anti-seize compound on them and only tighten to the manufacturer's recommended torque setting.

Chainring bolts should be tightened gradually and in sequence (that is, not from left to right but from opposite bolt to opposite bolt). This is so that you don't over-tighten them and to ensure that the rings run true. There's one set for the two large chainwheels and one set for the granny ring (if you have a triple).

Fitting chainrings

1 Chainrings will have an alignment arrow, which usually lines the chainrings up with the crank. Another giveaway to orientation on the outer (big) chainwheel is a chain pip – an aluminium grommet that stops the chain getting jammed between the spider and the crank, should the chain unship.

2 The inner chainwheel may also have an orientation mark (especially if it's on a triple crank, and the ring has grooves and ramps for the chain to shift along). Usually, the graphics on the outside of both chainrings will have been designed to line up. Once the rings are aligned, hold them together with the first bolt, as they're unlikely to be able to stay in place.

3 On Campagnolo Record cranks, one of the bolts threads directly into the crank arm. There's a spacer and a shim to provide exact alignment, so when reassembling them, place this bolt in first.

4 Use a decent-quality grease or copper slip on the bolts and bolt-holes. Not only does this prevent the bolts from seizing, but also stops them 'drying out' and creaking as time goes by.

5 Most chainring bolts take a 5mm Allen key and need to be tightened to 6Nm (aluminium) or 10Nm (steel).

6 Torque key fittings are now being used on new Campagnolo cranks, so make sure to use the right tools and carry them with you in your toolkit.

7 Chainring bolts can rotate in the crank, so use a bolt-wrench to hold the nut at the back and prevent it from spinning.

FAQ: What is the usual drive set-up on a road bike?

53/39 toothed chain rings are typical, but you'll find any number of combinations is possible on most cranks.

The Compact drive option

Compact drive is a very sensible option for anyone who likes riding a road bike for training and pleasure, but doesn't necessarily want to race. Indeed, many new bikes are now coming with a compact drive set-up as standard, and this is a welcome trend for riders who are more interested in riding 'comfortably' than they are about racing. It's all about having enough gears for the hills, so compact can help without adding extra weight.

It allows you to retain the clean road bike lines and keeps the bike looking less cluttered than with a triple set-up. Campagnolo and Shimano now offer triple groupsets at Record, Chorus and Dura-Ace, and Ultegra, but you have to ask yourself whether it's really necessary. Also, some frames struggle to accept a triple crank, as they've been designed specifically to be used with a double.

Ring sizes

The latest Compact road cranks have a 110mm PCD which means they can get down to a 34-tooth inner chainwheel.

Weight comparison

Generally speaking, a triple group weighs about 200g more than a standard double. There are too many variables, so a standard benchmark isn't really possible – but for example, the new Campagnolo Record Ultra-Torque Compact set-up (with double crank) is under 750g, while a good quality triple crank and BB will weigh around 1kg. This represents a 250g saving, which is about the weight of a front hub.

Gearing

Be honest, how often do you use 53 x 12 anyway? A 50 x 11 is still a massive gear in anyone's book – combine it with a 36-tooth inner chainring and a 11–25 cassette, and you'll be able to bomb up hills as well as down them. In fact, if you fit 50 x 11, you'll achieve a gear of 119in (302cm), which is a bigger gear than 53 x 12 at 116in (295cm).

Gear ratio range comparison (using 12–25 tooth cassette)

Gear length is measured by the distance a bike travels with one pedal revolution.

Double compact with 50/34 rings	35.7in–109.5in	(90.7cm–278.1cm)
Double 'Standard' with 53/39 rings	42.1in–119.3in	(106.9cm–303.0cm)
Triple with 52/42/30 rings	31.5in–113.9in	(80.0cm–289.3cm)

NB: It's worth noting that a double chainring set-up also allows more 'usable' gears than on a triple, i.e. gears which the chainline can handle more efficiently, while providing less doubling-up of ratios.

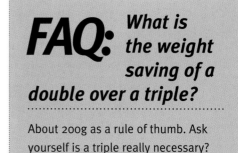

FAQ: What is the weight saving of a double over a triple?

About 200g as a rule of thumb. Ask yourself is a triple really necessary?

CARE & MAINTENANCE
Planning for a smooth, effective drivetrain

Front mech

Dropped chains can be a problem when using a compact drive system. A standard road front mech is designed with a larger plate-size, to be used with a 52/42 combination or the more popular 53/39. Campagnolo have a special front mech called the CT, and this is designed with a smaller inner plate so it shifts better and holds the chain on. However, the usual reason for a dropped chain is a poor chainline and badly matching components. Stick with one brand and keep things simple, without too many big jumps in gear sizes. Fitting a chain-retainer is a good idea. Usually called 'chain-watchers', they're plastic clips that sit inside the inner chainwheel where a hook prevents the chain from dropping. These devices are often used by pro mechanics when setting up odd gear ratios.

Rear mech capacity

This will depend on the ratios you're running on your cassette and chainrings. Most shifting problems start when the chain is placed under shifting pressure and the mech cannot cope with the pressure. Work the capacity out as follows:

11–25 cassette	(subtract 11 from 25)	= 14T
50/36 chainrings	(subtract 36 from 50)	= 14T

EDITOR'S TIP

"Personally I love the simplicity of the of the single fixing on Campagnolo's Ultra-Torque system"

Then add the two together – in this case, the total capacity required is 28 teeth.

The bigger the ratios, the longer the arm (or cage) of the rear mech you'll require – this allows for the slack in the longer chain to be accounted for by the arm. This is why triple set-ups need a long-arm mech to work properly with wide-ratio gears.

Shimano short-cage road mechs usually have a capacity of 29 teeth, which means you could run a 50/36 chainring and a 12–27 cassette. Campagnolo short-cage rear mechs can cope with 28 teeth, so they work best with a 50/36 crank and a 12–25 cassette. This will also cope with closer ratios, so if you wanted a racing ratio you could just swap the cassette for an 11–23, for example. I suggest that if you prefer Campagnolo and want to swap between cassette ratios, go for the mid-length mech as it can cope with 30 teeth (Campagnolo produce three types, and the longest has a capacity of 39 teeth).

KNOW HOW

The bottom bracket:
This is where most problems start. Don't compromise by trying to use what happens to be fitted, get the bottom bracket that the crank manufacturer recommends.

CHANGE & UPGRADE
Fitting cranks
The Campagnolo Ultra-Torque solution

Ultra-Torque cranks rely on an axle which joins in the centre of the BB axle. Like Shimano's, this is a very simple yet strong solution to fastening the cranks into the frame. The bearings are sealed and outboard of the frame, and they allow for an oversized-diameter axle for greater stiffness and efficiency. The whole unit is held in place with a 10mm Allen-key bolt located in the centre of the BB axle joining the two halves of the axle, which has a set of locking teeth to maintain a close join. This means that there's only one fixing for the whole system and ensures simplified fitting and ease of service. As with Shimano, the frame's BB shell needs to be tapped and faced, so as to offer exact fitting for the BB cups.

1 First, the BB cups install into the frame in the same way as Shimano's and using the same pattern spanner. Tighten to the cups to 35Nm.

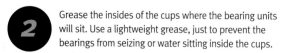

2 Grease the insides of the cups where the bearing units will sit. Use a lightweight grease, just to prevent the bearings from seizing or water sitting inside the cups.

3 The drive-side crank is inserted first. The bearing is factory-fitted to the inside of the cranks and this can be replaced.

4 Push the crank into the BB cups so that the bearing fits flush with the edge of the cups.

5 Once the drive-side bearing is in place, you can fit the spring clip – this prevents the drive side from falling out when you insert the left-hand crank.

6 Line up the left hand crank with the drive side crank – it's possible to fit the cranks 'wonky', as the serrated mating point is symmetrical.

7 As with the drive side, the left-hand-crank-side bearing fits flush with the BB cup and is sealed with a rubber seal.

8 Once lined up, it should be very easy to push the two crank sides together – the axle will mesh perfectly inside the BB shell.

9 Apply some grease to the thread of the bolt and, with a socket-set extension bar, pass the bolt into the hole on the drive side of the assembly, then locate the thread in the centre of the axle.

10 Tighten the bolt with a torque wrench. The correct tightening torque is 42Nm. To remove the cranks, simply undo this bolt and pull the left-hand crank away. Then remove the spring clip and remove the drive side.

CHANGE & UPGRADE
Fitting cranks

SRAM/Truativ cranks

1 SRAM cranks use a similar system to Shimano's, but like Campagnolo, it's a one-bolt-fitting unit. The cups fit in the same way and use the same pattern-spanner as Shimano and Campagnolo.

2 The axle is attached to the drive side and passes through the two cups. Apply a little grease to the parts that come into contact with the bearings.

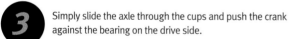

3 Simply slide the axle through the cups and push the crank against the bearing on the drive side.

4 There's an ISIS-style fitting on one end of the axle and this will protrude from the cups to allow the left-hand crank to tighten onto, and secure, the system in one action.

5 There's an aluminium sleeve on the inside of the left-hand crank, inside the carbon arm, which requires a little grease on the inside to prevent it from seizing.

6 There's a simple captive bolt on the left-hand crank, which tightens the whole system and also removes the crank in one, so as you undo the bolt the cranks will pull off the end of the axle.

CHANGE & UPGRADE
The bottom bracket
Servicing and fitting

Bottom bracket servicing and fitting

BBs come in a variety of lengths, sizes and specifications. They're either standard square-taper, ISIS, Octalink or 'through-axle' fittings like Campagnolo Ultra-Torque or Shimano Hollowtech II. (If you have a through-axle, turn to pages 169–70 for specific information on these types.)

Earlier versions, which used loose ball-bearing cup-and-axle, required attention even after the smallest rainfall. They also needed the patience of a watchmaker to set up without play or dragging. However, in recent years the one-piece unit with sealed bearings and a fiddle-free cartridge housing has been developed and can be set up to be smooth-running and trouble-free.

All types of English-threaded BB unit thread into the BB shell of the frame, with the right-hand cup threading in anti-clockwise (as it's a left-hand thread) and the left-hand cup threading in clockwise (as it's a standard, right-hand thread).

English or Italian?

The BB threads in most road bikes are 'English' pattern (marked '1.370in 24 TPI'). Some bikes (mainly Italian-brand road bikes) have 'Italian' threads (marked '36 24in'), which are slightly larger in diameter than the usual English bracket threads. Italian threads are also both right-hand threads on the drive and non-drive side.

Always check the size on the side of the bracket cups before you start to adjust.

Most standard Shimano units are sealed disposable units, which need completely replacing when they wear out. However, with a few more expensive brackets you can replace the bearings, in a similar way to cartridge-bearing hubs.

Square–taper BBs

On a square-taper BB, a two-degree angled taper is machined on four faces of the axle to give you a tight, precision fit into the square-tapered holes in the alloy cranks. This is a fairly standard engineering technique and gives a large contact area at the connection between the cranks and the axle. N.B. Check that the fit is correct for your crank when buying a new BB. The usual cause of creaking cranks is either dirt in this area, or an incompatible fit. Octalink and ISIS systems use a splined axle that is oversized and therefore less vulnerable to twisting forces than the standard square taper. They're also slightly lighter. However, they've now been superseded by the larger-diameter (and even lighter) through-axle cranks. However, many smaller brands still use ISIS and Octalink fittings and BBs. The central sleeve of a sealed BB keeps the bearings sealed from the water and dirt that can get into the inside of the BB via the frame tubes. The sleeve also acts as an accurate spacer to hold the cups and bearings in the correct position – they're usually made from aluminium or plastic. Lock-rings are not always necessary in modern cassette-type brackets, as they have a standard width fit.

Bolts and threads

The BB axle has threads tapped into either end of it for accepting the crank bolts. The crank bolts are normally Allen-key bolts set in plastic washers (to seal the crank extractor threads), or the captive bolt system, which enables the crank to be removed in the loosening action. Older cranks may have a 14mm or 15mm bolt, which requires a socket spanner to remove.

Standard Campagnolo square taper

Axle length

The axle length depends on the type of crank you're using. Standard BB axles come in a huge range of lengths, from 103mm to 124mm. When you replace a unit, always use the same-length axle. Shorter axles can mean that the chainrings rub on the frame, while longer ones will mess up your chainline and your gears won't work. If you're fitting a new crank and BB, check with the manufacturer which axle length you'll need to match your old set-up. If you ruin or cross-thread the threads in your BB, you can have it re-reamed and re-threaded to a larger size. A framebuilder can sometimes repair the threads too, but these jobs are best done by a qualified mechanic, as ruining the BB will usually mean your frame will be severely compromised and it'll be hard to service in the future.

Regardless of what type of drivetrain your bike has, failing to prepare the frame will mean that the BB unit won't sit properly in the bike. It may spin around okay, but once the cranks and chain are installed, a poorly prepared and fitted BB will damage the bearings, and the unit won't run efficiently.

Shimano Octalink

Fitting standard bottom brackets

1 Thread and BB preparation is essential. The tools needed to do this job are very expensive and require careful handling. This may mean you have to get a good bike shop to do the first few (cutting) tasks for you, but it's essential that the threads are cleaned and the faces squared up before you start.

3 The new unit will have one removable side, which is usually on the non-drive side. Pull this off, so that the unit can be installed into the drive side first. This side has a left-hand thread and tightens anti-clockwise.

2 The threads need to be thoroughly cleaned. Remove any oxide build-up and then dry off completely. Dress the threads with a good-quality grease – waterproof greases are best – and use copper slip on titanium components. Some mechanics will use thread-lock on Italian BBs to prevent the cups from loosening, but be careful, as this can create long-term problems.

4 The non-drive-side cup is right-hand-threaded and is designed to be flange-less, so it can accommodate a variety of widths of BB. This tightens clockwise and will mesh with the cartridge inside the shell. Again, tighten this with your fingers until there's 1cm (½in) of thread left showing. If the threads have been properly prepared, you'll be able to turn the unit into place with your fingers.

Creaking bottom bracket? Check it out and see if it needs replacing

✔ Check that the cranks are tight

✔ Check that the pedals are tight and that they have greased threads

✔ Check the chainring bolts are greased and tight

✔ Check the saddle and seatpost

✔ Check for corrosion and water in the frame's BB shell

✔ Strip the unit clean completely and reassemble with fresh grease

✔ Replace BB unit – re-tap threads and re-face frame

5 Shimano brackets use a special tool that sits in serrations around the edge of the cup. Some brackets use a set of holes that accept a pin spanner or peg tool and a lock-ring to hold it in position. If you don't get the right tools for the bracket, you risk making a mess of the unit and your frame.

EDITOR'S TIP *"If you ruin or cross thread your BB your frame will be severely compromised. Ask yourself is this a job for a qualified mechanic?"*

6 Campagnolo BBs have a smaller ring of serrations and use the same remover as their cassettes. Be careful with poorly fitting or worn tools, as these can easily be rounded out.

7 The best tool to remove Campagnolo BBs is one that can be threaded into the ends of the BB axle and held 'captive'. These are much safer and easier when exerting plenty of pressure to remove stubborn units. Holding everything firmly in position like this leaves you free to get on with the job.

8 Next, use the BB tool to tighten the unit into the frame. Make sure that the shoulder of the unit on the drive side is tight up against the frame first. This is to make sure that the chainset will sit in the right place to achieve the most efficient chainline. With the flange flush to the frame, it won't loosen off.

9 Once the drive side is tight, you can tighten the non-drive side and lastly tighten both side cups to 40–50Nm (NB: Check manufacturer's recommendation). Clean up any excess grease around the frame and threads, then you can re-install the cranks. Replace the cable guide (the bolt may need shortening if you've fitted a different type of bracket). Don't tighten this bolt into the outside of the unit as it can damage the seal.

KNOW HOW

Bottom brackets

Most of the older bottom bracket systems seem to be in the process of being superseded by the large diameter through-axle crank type.

Road chains

Bicycle chain drive is incredibly efficient under tough conditions

Chains – replacement and care

Chains are designed to wear out. They're incredibly efficient, but have to put up with a lot of abuse, and the constant twisting and shifting up and down the sprockets wears the average road bike chain out in a matter of months. Finer 10-speed chains also require a fair amount of careful cleaning and lubricating. There's also a variation in quality of chain. Plated chains are the best, as they're less likely to corrode and therefore last longer and shift better than a plain steel chain. Stainless steel and even titanium chains are also available – they may well last a little longer than plain steel chains but, as they're harder, they can wear aluminium chainrings if they aren't regularly cleaned and lubricated.

Replacing an old, worn-out chain usually requires replacing the cassette as well – as the chain stretches, it wears the cassette sprockets too, turning the whole drivetrain into scrap metal. This can be expensive, so using a cheap chain and replacing it often – rather than buying an expensive chain and waiting until it wears out the sprockets and chainring too – will turn out cheaper in the long run.

The chain is made up of side plates (external links) and internal links with rollers inside them. The rollers assist in the smooth running of the gearing and pedal action.

Checking a chain for wear

1 Measure across 24 links of the chain – it should measure 12in. If it's more than that, the chain has stretched beyond a usable length. A chain in this state will start to wear other components and shifting will become increasingly erratic.

2 There are several chain-measuring devices, but the Park one pictured here is the best one around. Place the two pins into the links and turn the dial to ascertain how much stretch there is in the links. If the dial is in the red, the chain has stretched beyond serviceable life.

3 To check the chain and the chainrings for wear, put the chain on the biggest chainring and smallest cassette sprocket. If you can pull the chain off the chainring and it can clear the tip of one of the chainring teeth, or the chain moves excessively at the top and bottom of the chainring, this means the chain may need to be replaced.

UPGRADE...
Jockey Wheels
Ceramic jockey wheels have a certain wow factor. They're practical too, offering less resistance in the drivetrain.

Shimano 9- and 10-speed chains
Installing a new Shimano chain requires special joining pins

1 This darker-coloured, flat-ended pin marks the spot where the chain was first joined. If you're removing the chain to clean it and have a new link to rejoin the chain, find this link and break the chain exactly opposite it.

2 Remove the old chain and measure the new one next to it. Depending on the type of chain, you'll have to remove a certain number of links from one end. Leave the 'open' plates or external link end (seen here on the right) and remove links from the other end, leaving internal links ready for rejoining. This keeps the factory-fitted end complete.

3 Thread the new chain through the rear mech jockey wheels and over the chainwheel. Don't put it back on the chainring until you've joined the chain, as the slack will make it easier to rejoin the two ends. The Shimano chain is joined with this special pin to make sure that the link is pushed in the correct way. Grease the pin so that it'll go in easily.

4 Push the link through using a quality Shimano-chain-compatible chain-rivet tool. This Park tool has shaped jaws to prevent the side plates becoming squeezed together. Keep the chain straight and turn the handle firmly and slowly to make sure that the pin goes through totally straight.

5 The Park chain tool is set up so that it stops once the link is in place (there's a circlip on the threaded shaft that prevents you going too far). There's a definite click as the pin passes through the link. At that point, back off the handle and check that the pin is in place.

6 Although Shimano 10-speed chains use the same principles as a nine-speed chain, they're noticeably narrower and they use a specific 10-speed pin (rivet).

7 For 10-speed chains make sure that you use a genuine HG tool and that the pin is always pushed through from the outside. Check that the pin protrudes an equal distance either side of the plates.

8 When the Shimano (nine- or 10-speed) pin is through to the other side and the fatter part of the pin is equally spaced on either side of the link plates, snap off the guide with some pliers. Obviously, you need to do this before you check the gears are working.

9 Once the pin is in place there may be a little stiffness in the link, which may jump as you pedal the gears backwards. To remove a stiff link, first add some lube to it and push it into an inverted V-shape.

10 Then place your thumbs on the links to either side of this link. Grip the chain and very gently push the chain against itself. This very careful 'twisting' should free the link immediately.

SRAM 10-speed chains
A different approach with a very handy quick release link

SRAM chains

SRAM chains started off life as Sachs/Sedis, two massive European chain manufacturers. Their expertise resulted in perhaps the best shifting and most reliable chains on the market. SRAM now own these companies and they've created the easiest-to-install 10-speed-system chain to date, and this is used in their Force and Rival Road race groupsets.

All nine- and 10-speed SRAM chains come with 'quick-release' links called Power Links. They can fix a chain without the need for tools and are really handy to use for emergencies – so carry one in your roadside tool kit. They're easy to install and save you messing about with chain tools every time you want to take off a chain.

To remove them, simply take the tension off the chain (I find it best to take the chain off the chainrings first) and push the links against each other and your hands towards one another at the same time. It takes practice, but is a great way to remove your chain for washing. Ten-speed Power Links can't be removed and a new link has to be used once the chain has been broken.

1 To get the correct chain length, measure the chain so that it's tight when placed from biggest sprocket to biggest chainring, bypassing the rear mech (it's easiest to do this before the rear mech is attached).

2 Then add two links to this length. Bear in mind that fitting Power Links requires removing the side plates from both ends of the chain so they join the chain between two rollers.

5 Then install the rear mech and thread the chain though the jockey wheels over the chainrings and through the front mech, join the two open ends of chain with the Power Link and slot the pins into place – they'll sit halfway, not quite bedded into the closed position.

6 Use the crank arm and brace the rear wheel so that you can 'snap' the Power Link into place – it'll seat into place, and the main advantage is that no tools are required and it's impossible to get a stiff link.

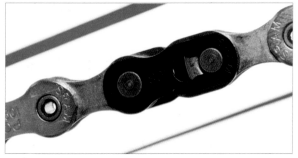

7 Once the Power Link is in place, you'll have to break the chain next time opposite this link and use a new Power Link each time you rejoin the chain. SRAM chains are supplied with spare Power Links.

KNOW HOW

Chain technology:
Campagnolo pioneered the 10-speed chain and shifting system in 1999. The chain has been through several changes over the past few years resulting in the Campagnolo Record Ultra Narrow chain.

Chainline:
The ideal line for the chain is parallel to the centre line of the bike, which passes from the centre of the rear hub to the centre of the bottom bracket when the chain is on the middle ring at the front and around the centre of the rear sprockets. To achieve it you have to have the correct bottom bracket axle length.

Chainslap:
The annoying sound of the chain tap-dancing on your chainstay paintwork, usually heard when travelling at speed or out of control over rough ground.

Chain suck:
The result of worn chainrings - the chain remains stuck to the 'back-side' of the chainring and becomes lodged in the frame and crank. Can damage paint work and stop you dead.

EDITOR'S TIP

"Using a cheap chain and replacing it often will turn out cheaper in the long run"

Campagnolo 10-speed chains
The ultra narrow Record chain requires careful installation

1 The 10-speed Campagnolo chain has a serial number stamped on the external link. This is very important, as it denotes the link that needs to be left untampered. The external links are designed to face a certain way to accept the countersunk pin that joins the two ends of chain together.

2 A Campagnolo 10-speed HD chain-pin has a detachable guide pin and a hollow rivet – this guide pin simply slots into the rivet and can be taken out once the chain has been joined.

3 The HD pin is always placed on the inside of the drivetrain, so as to be pushed outwards of the bike (for the reason explained in step 1).

4 Measure the chain in the small sprocket and inner chainwheel. When the chain ends are pulled together you're looking for a gap of 15mm between the chainline along the bottom and the top of the lower jockey wheel.

The Drivetrain

1 The rear mech should just take up the slack in the chain, and the chain should run clear of the jockey-wheel-cage guides (the tab at the rear of this cage).

2 Place the chain on the big ring and link up the chain with the connecting pin. Join the chain under the chainring from the inside out – double-check that you have the stamped external plate on the outside before you do this.

3 The Campagnolo chain tool has a locking pin that pushes across the internal and external links to ensure that the chain is held tightly and the links are perfectly aligned.

4 It may appear over-complicated, but special 'HD Link' rejoining links are required if the chain is broken and needs to be rejoined. Measure the same length of links and remove the same amount from the chain opposite the first join. This can then be installed with two HD pins.

Chain tips

✔ For the best results, replace your chain every 2000–3000km (1250–1850mi). This will prevent wear to the cassette sprockets, chainrings and mechs.

✔ Swap steel rings for aluminium ones and replace them at least every one to two years. Make sure that you use 10-speed compatible chainrings and mechs, as they too are designed to work only with narrow chains.

✔ Buy a chain bath and clean your chain once a week.

✔ De-grease and thoroughly clean a new chain before using it. They're packed in grease for storage to stop them from rusting, but this just attracts dirt. Run the chain through a chain bath and re-lubricate with a quality chain lube. This will keep your new chain clean for longer.

✔ A chain 'jumps' when there's something worn in the drivetrain. Usually, if you fit a new chain it'll skip over the cassette sprockets in some ratios, which means that the cassette needs replacing too. However, there may be a stiff link.

✔ If you want to experiment with chain lengths, do so with an old chain. You can then run through the gears and decide on the final length before you cut a new one and measure it next to the old one.

The mountain bike drivetrain

Bigger, tougher, heavier, more...

Built for climbing mountains and screaming back down in a flurry of flying rock and shale, the mountain bike drivetrain has to be super tough and deliver stump-pulling traction to the rider. Speed is not the first priority on an MTB so triple chainsets with a wide range of gears are the norm. How many of the gears are actually useful is a topic of café debate, but you will rarely find a mountain biker taking the trouble to revert to a double chainring.

Types and styles

The bottom bracket and crank fitting systems on an MTB are pretty much the same as for road bikes Square-taper, Octalink, ISIS and so on are all represented. But, as on the road, a newish design is starting to predominate – the through axle style.

Worth fitting yourself?

Fitting a standard MTB bottom bracket is a similar process to that described for road bikes. And the same caveats apply. You are warned that a bottom bracket may not sit correctly unless the frame is properly prepared. The threads of the bottom bracket shell (the hole at the bottom of the frame where the bottom bracket sits) should be tapped. The faces of the shell should be 'faced', which means cut so they are absolutely flat and parallel to one another. The tools required to do this are quite expensive and require careful handling so it is always suggested you get a bike shop to do this part. And well, by the time you've booked your bike in and got a slot, you might well feel 'let them do the lot!'

The bottom bracket

The bottom bracket unit screws into the bottom bracket shell. The unit has one removable side, usually on the non-drive side. With this removed, install the unit into the drive side first – it has a left-hand thread and tightens anti-clockwise. The non-drive side cup installs clockwise and meshes with the unit inside the shell.

CHANGE & UPGRADE
Integrated BB servicing
The Shimano Hollowtech II system is becoming a firm favourite

The Shimano Hollowtech II Crank setup is very easy to install and service. It takes its design influence from the Aheadset – basically, it's an oversize tube secured at either end with the cranks, just like your forks are held in place with the stem. The system is known as a through axle or integrated crank.

The drive side will sit perfectly flush to the frame, so the chainline will be spot-on for Shimano drive systems (derailleurs, chains and cassettes). Chainrings are replaced in the same way as any crank.

The bearings in the bottom bracket unit are spaced further apart and outside the frame's bottom bracket shell, allowing for a larger axle diameter and a much stiffer crankset than you would get on a square taper, an Octalink or an ISIS splined type. Many other crank manufacturers, including Bontrager, Truvativ, Race Face and DMR, have adopted this type of system for strength and reliability. The result is better functionality for one of the weakest points of a bike's drivetrain.

Tools required:

- in-line taps
- facing tool (N.B. If you don't have a facing tool, you will need the bike shop to do some of the preparatory work for you. The bottom bracket has to be properly faced for it to work properly.)
- Shimano C-spanner TL-FC32 (supplied with bottom bracket)
- Shimano axle-bolt tool TL-FC16 (supplied with bottom bracket)
- Allen keys
- torque wrench
- grease (Shimano Anti-Seize is good)

 Face the bracket shell on both sides. This must be done before the bearing unit can be set up properly. Because the bearings are placed on the outside of the frame's bottom bracket shell and they have to be parallel, you need a flat, very clean bracket. You will find that some frames need more preparation than others. Clean out any swarf from the bottom bracket and use some Shimano anti-seize grease on the threads.

 Spacers are needed and are placed on the drive side. This ensures the correct spacing and correct chainline is maintained for efficient shifting. Measure the width of the bottom bracket shell – it will be either 68 mm or 73 mm. The number of spacers needed depends on the width of the bottom bracket: three spacers are required for a 68 mm bottom bracket shell (one on the left-hand cup); two spacers are required for a 68 mm bottom bracket shell and bracket-type front mech (one on either side); one spacer is required for a 73 mm bottom bracket shell (on the right-hand side); no spacers are required for a 73 mm bottom bracket shell and bracket-type fitting front mech.

3 Fit the internal plastic cover to the right (drive) side cup and thread it into the bottom bracket shell. Once again, remember that the drive side is a left-hand thread (turns anti-clockwise) and the non-drive side is a right-hand thread (turns clockwise). At this stage, do not tighten the cups completely, just finger-tighten both cups into place.

4 It's best to locate the left side cup (right-hand thread – clockwise) before you tighten the right side cup completely, as the plastic sleeve has to mate with both cups inside the bottom bracket shell. Once they are both flush with the edge of the bottom bracket, tighten them to 35–50 Nm using the C-spanner, which is usually supplied with the unit.

5 The right-hand crank and bottom bracket axle are fixed as a 'one-piece' complete unit. Push the axle into the bottom bracket cups all the way, a gentle tap with the flat of your hand will make sure it is in the right position. There is a flat surface on the inside of the crank that has to sit flush with the outside face of the bearing, so make sure that you can't see a gap between the crank and the bottom bracket bearing face.

6 There are two rubber O-rings that fit over the crank axle to seal the bearing units. One has to be installed on the drive side, the other before the left-hand crank is added. Wet these seals with some grease so they slip over the axle easily.

7 There are two flat sections on the splined axle, which self-locate into the crank so that the cranks line up perfectly. The crank won't go on any other way, so don't try to force it. Push the crank on the axle and place a hand on each crank and push them firmly together. This will check that they are both seated correctly with the cranks tight up against the bearing cups.

8 There is a cap to thread into the open end of the left-hand crank axle which tightens the two cranks onto the bearings. The cap only needs to be 'finger tight' to take up the play, but there is a special Shimano or Park tool to help tighten this cap.

9 Lastly, tighten the two Allen bolts on the left hand crank arm evenly; do them up alternately and a little at a time until you reach the recommended tightening torque of 10–15 Nm. The cranks should spin freely.

10 Removing the crank-set is simple. It requires no special crank pullers or spanners – just undo the fixing bolts and the cap and pull the left-hand crank off. However, if you do remove the unit make sure that you follow steps 7–9 in order to reinstall it correctly.

CHANGE & UPGRADE
Cranks and chainrings

Removing MTB cranks, setting chainlines and fitting chainrings

1 On standard cranks, the fixing bolt has an 8 mm Allen head with the washer as an integral part of the bolt. The black plastic washer pictured here acts as a dust cover to keep dirt out of the threads. Old-style cranks still use a 14 or 15 mm hex-headed bolt and washer protected by a separate dust cap.

2 Once you have removed the bolts and washers, remove the crank using a crank puller. This tool is essential for taking the cranks off the bike, and good ones won't damage the threads or the end of the axle. Clean out any mud from the crank threads with a squirt of spray lube. Thread the crank puller into the crank as far as it will go, then undo the centre bolt first so it fits as flush as possible, being careful to get it in straight. N.B. ISIS and Octalink cranks require a larger head on the crank pulling tool.

3 Once you have correctly inserted the puller, tighten the arm towards the bottom bracket axle. The arm rests on the end of the axle and the pushing/pulling motion forces the crank off the square axle taper. The crank will then drop off on the floor, so be careful to keep hold of it. N.B. If you only insert the crank puller in by a few threads, or cross-thread it, it will strip out the threads. Once the threads are stripped your crank will be useless.

4 Always retighten cranks to the recommended torque setting and check them after the first ride as they can loosen off due to the pedalling force.

5 ISIS axles have a symmetrical splined pattern on the axle and it's worth cleaning this every time you remove the crank arms. Shimano Octalink cranks are very different so don't try to mix them up.

6 The chainline tool assesses the correct spacing of the bottom bracket axle and the alignment of the cassette sprockets with the chainrings. There should be a straight line between the middle chainring and the middle sprocket of the cassette.

7 For ideal shifting you really want the chain to be at it's straightest in the middle chainring and in the middle of the cassette, allowing for optimum spread of gears with less chain angle. This improves shifting, prolongs the life of the chain and prevents it from unshipping unexpectedly.

8 Fitting chainrings is very simple, but make sure that you get the correct size for your crank. Use a decent copper slip on the bolts and bolt holes. Not only does this prevent the bolts from seizing, but it also stops them 'drying out' and creaking as time goes by.

9 Chainring bolts can rotate in the crank, so use a bolt wrench to hold the nut at the back to prevent it from spinning.

10 The spider is the central yoke that attaches the rings to the cranks. It's important for two reasons: first, it's responsible for the accurate alignment of the rings to the rear cassette (chainline); and second, it needs to be super stiff and totally flex free. Most spiders can be removed from the crank and replaced if they are bent or twisted. The DMR Chieftain crank shown here has a split ring on the inside of the lock ring to prevent it from loosening.

11 Use this Shimano lock ring tool to remove the lock ring. This is the industry standard for most crank spider lock rings. Hold the tool in a vice or use a large spanner.

12 Lock rings are usually factory fitted and therefore very tight, so be careful not to slip. Some Race Face cranks have replaceable spider arm ends and Shimano cranks all bolt to one chainring. However, you do need to know how to replace the chainrings and spider should you crash into a log and bend the whole lot.

Gear Systems

Making the fullest use of mechanical advantage

At the beginning of cycling history, the only way you could get more travel for every turn of your legs was to put a bigger diameter wheel in your penny farthing. Back then, your top speed was limited by your inside leg measurement. The chain and sprocket ended that problem, bringing in the safety bicycle, and the derailleur system allowed riders the luxury of ten speeds.

That used to be the pinnacle of bicycle technology, but the improvement to hubs and mechs have made bigger ratios and a wider spread of gears easily available. Nowadays most new road bikes come with 18 to 30 gear ratios. Modern derailleur cassettes and chains work smoothly and shift crisply as a result of being complicated and finely engineered, which you can also read as being susceptible to wear and tear. They also use alloys to save weight, which

"Modern gears work smoothly and shift crisply as a result of being finely engineered, which also means being susceptible to wear and tear"

wear quicker, so mountain bikers will be changing cassettes more often. Like road riders who change them also for different sorts of riding, racing, training, touring and so on. Luckily modern systems make that comparatively easy.

Shimano Index System

How the most used mountain bike gear system is installed and works

Shimano saw the potential of the mountain bike almost from the beginning of mass manufacture and their indexed system (using a ratchet in the gear lever which pulls or releases enough cable in one click to hop the chain one gear) still dominates the sector. There have been many developments of the system, but the basic principles remain much the same.

Tools:
- Screwdriver
- Teflon lube

1 To replace the inner gear cable, find the window on the shifter. This is usually a cross-head plug. To thread the cable through the window, place the gear shifter in the highest position. You will be able to see the white plastic cable carrier. In this position the cable can be pushed through easily. The screw plug must be replaced after the cable has been threaded through as it prevents muck getting into the system and ruining the mechanism.

2 Gear cables have a smaller nipple than brake cables and they are thinner (1.2 mm). A squirt of Teflon lube on the cable is a good idea, as it will keep the cables loose running.

3 The rear mech needs to be installed onto the gear hanger. Check that the hanger is straight and that the threads are clean and uncrossed. The rear gear has to hang perfectly straight. If the hanger is bent or the derailleur cage is twisted, the system will not work.

4 The inner wire is clamped onto the rear mech by a washer. To see how this works, look for a channel moulded onto the body of the mech – the washer will be marked where the cable has been.

Hub gears

Utility bike riders skip around the whole process of pushing the chain from sprocket to sprocket by using hub gears, which now come with five and seven speeds as well as in the venerable Sturmey Archer three-speed form. Not much maintenance needed there. But if you really want to keep things simple there is the single-speed hub, or the fixed gear single-speed hub which shoves technology back 100 years in the search for minimalism.

5 Screw the gear barrel adjuster fully in, so that there will be plenty of adjustment available when setting the cable. If all the cable outer sections are properly inserted and the gear shifter is in the highest gear position, it should be possible to pull the cable tight enough with your hand. Pull the cable in the direction of the channel you have identified in step 4. Lock it off.

6 Rear mechs work best with free-running jockey wheels. These can be replaced when the plastic wheels wear out. This improves shifting and helps keep the chain in contact with the sprockets on the cassette.

7 To replace the jockey wheels, remove the pivot screws. If you haven't done this before, paying attention to how it goes back together. Take a photo of the mech from both angles before you remove the bolts. The bush should be in the centre of the wheel.

8 This is the bottom jockey wheel from a Shimano XT rear mech. The bushes are made from a ceramic material so they do not rust up. The top jockey wheel has a sealed bearing in it. It is worth stripping and reassembling both wheels. Clean them completely and reassemble, using a Teflon lubricant.

9 Make sure that the jockey wheel is replaced so that it rotates in the right direction. There is usually an arrow on the plastic part of the wheel to help you do this. Once you have reassembled the cage, check that the top and bottom fixing screws are tight.

10 Adjust the limit screw marked 'H' when the chain is in the smallest sprocket. It is important that the chain can run smoothly over the sprocket and that the chain cannot move any further down the block. If this happens, the chain may become trapped between the frame and the cassette and jam up.

FAQ: *Why do perfect-shifting gears gradually go out of whack?*

It's almost always because the cable stretches and needs adjusting or replacing.

11 Next, adjust the limit screw marked 'L' when the gear is in the largest sprocket (lowest gear). Don't worry too much about the indexing working too well at this point, as you need to set the throw of the mech before tweaking the gears. Double-check that the chain can reach this sprocket, but also that the chain cannot jump over the top of the cassette and into the wheel. Also check that the mech cannot hit the spokes of the wheel. This can be disastrous!

12 The best way to check your indexing is to hold the back wheel off the ground in a work stand, leaving your hands free to pedal the bike and adjust the cable tension. Start by running through each gear and listening for any noise as you change up the gears, going from the smallest cog to the largest one. Check how easily the chain skips the gears – if it struggles to make the next sprocket then the cable is too loose, so you will need to tighten the cable by screwing the barrel adjuster anti-clockwise. Now change back down the gears (large to small cog) and check if there is a delay in the shift or if the chain stays stuck in one gear – if so, the cable is too tight and you will need to loosen it by turning the adjuster clockwise.

KNOW HOW

Rapid-rise rear mechs
Some Shimano gear systems use the rapid-rise system. This is a reverse shifting system and is designed to place less strain on the gears and provide a quicker shift. Adjustment for this system (on XTR) is done at the lever. The principle is exactly the same as above, but I find standard shifting mechs easier to adjust with the adjuster set on the drivetrain.

Stretching the cables

Once the gears are adjusted and working properly, you need to stretch the cables. Place the gear in the highest position and identify the rear gear cable on the top tube. Tighten the cable clamp to ensure it will not pull through. Grab the inner cable firmly in the centre of the open run on the top tube. Pull the cable gently but firmly upwards a couple of times. This will seat the outer cables in place and bed the whole cable run into place. Then readjust the gear system as in steps 11 and 12.

If the shift is still bad it may be due to one of the following problems:

1. The gear hanger is bent
2. The chain is too long or too short
3. The cables are old or there is a kink or obstruction somewhere in the run
4. The chain or sprockets are worn out
5. The cable is clamped into the rear gear in the wrong place

UPGRADE...
Chains
....
Chains are subject to wear and need to be changed. Give longevity to your drivetrain and reduce resistance by investing in better quality.

CHANGE & UPGRADE
Mountain bike-type gear cables

Cables are the key to sweet changing gears. Change them regularly and keep them well lubricated for great results...

Gear cables are the one element in the gear system that must be friction-free at all times. To keep a smooth-running gear cable you need regular check-ups and plenty of lubrication, and replacing the cables regularly will make your bike shift better and protect the levers from extra wear and tear. The gear cable outer has to be in top condition for the index system to work properly, so always check the cables after crashes as they are very brittle and vulnerable to cracking.

The secret to good-quality cabling is a very good-quality (sharp) set of cable cutters. Only use your cable cutters for cables, not for spokes and small bolts! The easiest way to measure outer cable lengths is to use the old bits of outer cable as cutting templates. The cables should be long enough that they don't snag or pull taut when the handlebars are fully rotated. Over-long cables flap about, which is both inefficient and dangerous.

Tools:
- cable cutters
- grease
- lightweight lubricant
- pointed 'podger' or 'bradawl' (used for making screw holes in wood)

1 Proper cable cutting is the first step in making your gears work correctly. Gear cables have a very brittle plastic outer casing, which can be damaged or cracked by using the wrong cutters when cutting them to length. Use cable shears that slice through the cable rather than pliers or cutters that just crush the casing.

2 The gear cable is different from the brake cable in that it is made up of strands that travel the length of the cable, inside which is a nylon liner that the gear cable can run through. These strands transfer all the effort from the gear shift into bracing the inner cable (or wire). This pulls on the derailleur and in turn pushes the chain onto the next sprocket or chainring.

3 Cutting the outer cable crimps the cable liners, closing up the hole that the inner wire has to go through. Use a bradawl or a podger to make the hole in the liner big enough for the inner wire to pass through unhindered. This reduces the friction on the cable and enables you to run the inner wires through easily once the cable ferrules are in place.

4 Outer cable ferrules must be applied to the end of each cable outer run. Cables without ferrules will fray and crack at the ends and the cracks will travel up the cable, which doesn't do much for your gear shift and allows water to get into the cable. Eventually, the cable strands will push their way through the cable guides and the whole system will pack up. I prefer plastic ferrules as they do not rust and are less likely to seize into the cable guides.

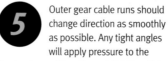

5 Outer gear cable runs should change direction as smoothly as possible. Any tight angles will apply pressure to the inner wire and therefore add friction. This slows the shift and can cause the gears to jump. On suspension bikes it is especially important to make sure that these runs are unhindered and have enough space to move as the bike moves.

6 Apply a small smear of grease to the ferrule before you push it into the cable stop or guide. This will make it easier to adjust the cable at the derailleur and also prevent it from getting stuck or seized up.

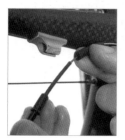

7 There is a seal on the final run of cable to the rear derailleur. This is designed to prevent water from running down the cable and into this very sensitive area. Unprotected sections will allow water in and eventually rust the inner wire and dry the outer cable so that the whole lot seizes up.

8 To release the cable from slotted cable guides, place the derailleur in the lowest gear (on the largest sprocket at the back). Then stop pedalling the drive and release the downshift lever completely. This will slacken the cable completely so you can release it.

9 The rubber shield shown here covers the adjusting screw on Shimano XT rear derailleurs. It prevents the adjuster from filling up with water and seizing up. You can still adjust the gears with this in place. The final run of outer needs to allow the rear derailleur to travel across all the gears. Allow enough for the gear to be in top and bottom without pulling on the cable or leaving a huge loop of outer.

10 The last run of cable to the rear derailleur is shown here with the rubber covers and weather guards in place. There should be enough cable for the derailleur to move unhindered. Most rear derailleurs pivot around the fixing bolt, so the cable has to be able to move with it. With a short cable, problems will arise as you shift into the lower gears, and the shift will be generally tight at the lever.

11 Lastly, remember to protect the frame and the paintwork from the outer cables, as vibrations from the trail will cause the cable to wear away at the frame. Place frame stickers where the cables rub, particularly by the handlebars but also at any point where a cable touches the frame. These sticky protectors will protect the cable from wearing through too.

EDITOR'S TIP *"Time spent on your gear cables is well spent. You could have 27 gears, all but three depending on cable length."*

CHANGE & UPGRADE
Mountain bike-front derailleur

Also known as the 'front mech', the front derailleur is steam-age engineering but it's light and it works...

There are a variety of front derailleur (or mech) fittings. Derailleur is the official name for these components, but most people call them mechs – so that's the term that I'll use here. Mechs are essentially guide plates for the chain that allow it to be moved onto the next chainwheel. Most fit to the seat tube with a clamp. However, some Shimano mechs fit onto the bottom bracket shell and behind the bracket cups. This type of mech is popular on frames that have complicated or interrupted seat tubes – usually on suspension bikes.

Shimano have perfected this mechanism to be 'indexed', so now one click at the lever allows for one chainring shift at the cranks. At least, that's the theory. Using the front mech properly takes practice, and you can only do this if it has been set up well in the first place. Setting it up also takes time and practice. It's a

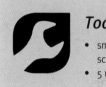

Tools:
• small cross-head screwdriver
• 5 mm Allen keys

very dynamic mechanism so it does require patience to get it perfect. Height, angle and throw are all influencing factors.

The plates are shaped so that they will not rub on the chain when they are set correctly, and so that they can pick up the chain and carry it to the next chainring. For many mechanics, the front mech is their biggest headache.

1 Angle the mech so that it is exactly parallel with all three chainrings. When you buy a new front mech it should have a small plastic spacer inside the mechanism. Do not pull this out as it is there to help you set the position and height of the mech. It allows you to align the outside plate of the mech with the outer (biggest) chainring and position the mech over the middle chainring. If you can't get the mech into this position, you may have problems with the chainline and you may need a different length bottom bracket.

2 If the angle is slightly out (as shown here), the shifting will be sloppy, so make sure you set the angle carefully. Spend time getting this bit right as it will have the biggest influence on the performance of the mech. If it is angled too far outwards it will foul on the crank when the pedals are turned.

3 The distance between the outside mech plate and the teeth of the chainring should be no more than 2–3 mm. This will ensure that the mech is correctly positioned to cope with the difference in size of the granny (smallest) ring and big ring. It also allows for the chain pick-up and will happily clear the teeth of the chainrings.

4 A good chainline is imperative; make sure that the chain can access all of the rear sprockets when in the middle chainring. You can also see that the mech in this position is exactly in line with the outer (big) chainring.

5 This full suspension bike needs a higher fitting mech (the clamp is further up the seat tube). However, the steps for adjusting it remain the same, and the space between the cage plate and the chainring is identical.

6 Next, attach the gear cable. Make sure that the gear shifter is in its lowest position so the cable is at its slackest. In this position the front mech will be over the granny ring. Pull the cable through the clamp firmly. Trap the cable in the clamp and check that it's in the right place, as this can affect the shift. Once the cable is pulled through and set you can adjust the low-limit stop screw.

7 Adjust the limit screw marked 'L' first. Place the rear mech in the biggest sprocket (lowest/ easiest gear), as this is the furthest the chain will travel. Then set the front mech so it only just clears the inside of the plate. In the granny ring you will probably only use three or four of the lowest gears, so make sure that these are working properly and then shift into the biggest chainring.

EDITOR'S TIP A plastic tyre lever jammed (carefully) into the parallelogram mechanism can simulate the 'setup' spacer and will also allow you two hands to adjust the fastening bolt and the mech angle.

 Now you can adjust the limit screw marked 'H'. Put the chain onto the big chainring (this may over-shift at first) and work the rear mech through all the gears. You will notice that the chain changes angle considerably, but it will cope with most of the gears on this chainring. Set the limit screw so that in the smallest rear sprocket it just clears the chain.

 On a full suspension bike this adjustment can be very tricky. Here the swing arm is in the way of the adjustment screws, so you would need to use a longer screwdriver. However, you can see that the plate of the front mech is set so that the chain is not rubbing even in the largest size sprocket at the rear.

Causes of front mech rubbing

If your front mech is rubbing, it will be due to one of the following problems:

1. The cable is too tight or too loose
2. The limit screws are incorrectly adjusted
3. The angle of the mech to the chainrings is wrong
4. The chainline is incorrect

Causes of unshipping a chain

If you have problems with the chain unshipping, it will be caused by one of the following:

1. The low adjust is set incorrectly, so you will have to push the mech further out with the limit screw
2. The chain is jumping over the top of the biggest chainring, so you will need to push the mech further in with the limit screw

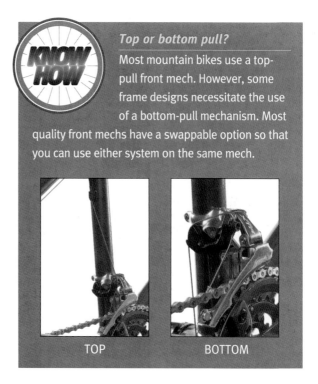

KNOW HOW

Top or bottom pull?
Most mountain bikes use a top-pull front mech. However, some frame designs necessitate the use of a bottom-pull mechanism. Most quality front mechs have a swappable option so that you can use either system on the same mech.

TOP   BOTTOM

SRAM Index System

Now a viable alternative to Shimano, SRAM gear systems work differently but just as well

Gripshift has been a viable alternative to Shimano for well over ten years. Now known as SRAM, the company makes a wide range of shifters and gear mechanisms for use with pretty much all makes of mountain bike gear system. SRAM can be used with either a Shimano HG or SRAM chains and either Shimano or SRAM ESP rear mechs. SRAM gear systems will handle cassette ratios of 11:28 to 14:34 and chainring combinations of 22/32/42, 24/34/46 and 26/36/46 or 48. The main difference between Shimano and SRAM rear mechs is that SRAM cannot use the sprung-pivot fixing bolt that Shimano can. This is at the bolt and gives you the advantage of a mechanism that moves as you shift between the chainrings. It's no better or worse than Shimano, just different.

Gripshift

SRAM's Gripshift system is a viable alternative to Shimano gears. The twist-grip gear shifter is simple and easy to service, and many cross-country racers prefer this system for its light weight and simple operation. Their 1:1 gearshift ratio makes the action very light and

Tools:
- pointed bradawl or small screwdriver
- Allen key
- cable cutters
- pliers

precise. Now SRAM have made trigger shifters and front derailleurs so you can have a non-Shimano-equipped bike with the disc brake of your choice. For the mechanic, the main advantage of this system is that Gripshift shifters are very simple to service and can easily be rebuilt.

1 Fit the Gripshifter so that there is plenty of room for grips and bar ends. Be careful not to over-tighten the fixing bolts as they can break the fixing clamp very easily. Also, be careful not to jam the gear adjuster behind the brake lever – position it so that it is protected from impact by the brake lever housing.

2 Gear cable replacement is relatively straightforward with all Gripshift shifters. First, place the gear selector in the highest gear (marked 7, 8 or 9 depending on how many gears you have) and pick out the rubber cover plate from the body of the shifter to reveal the nipple at the end of the gear cable.

3 The gear cable nipple is trapped behind a retaining plate and will need to be poked out with a pointed bradawl or small screwdriver. You may have to jiggle the twist grip a little to persuade it to come out.

4 SRAM's paddle-type shifters are similar in fitting to Shimano. They have Allen bolts sensibly placed on the top of the handlebar, which makes them very easy to install and adjust. Position them tight up behind the brake lever, but be careful not to obstruct the barrel adjuster.

5 Measure and cut a length of cable for the front shifter and the rear mech. SRAM rear mechs do not pivot with a spring at the fixing bolt, so getting the cable length spot-on is critical. The cable enters the mech from the front. Check the manufacturer's instructions for recommended lengths.

6 Adjust the limit screw marked 'H' for the highest gear setting to align the top pulley (or jockey) wheel with the outside edge of the smallest sprocket.

7 Then adjust the setting marked 'L'. However, this time align the top jockey wheel with the dead centre of the largest sprocket. Check that the mech cannot hit the spokes.

8 Now you can install the chain and place the mech in the smallest cog and granny (smallest) chainring. In this position, adjust the chain gap with the screw at the back of the mech – the distance between the top pulley and the sprocket should be 6 mm.

9 Pull the cable tight with a pair of pliers as you fix it in place. As with Shimano, do this in the highest gear setting on the shifter and check that the adjuster is wound in to allow more room for adjustment.

10 Pull the cable through the rear cable run and over the fin at the back of the mech, and attach it in the correct side of the fixing bolt. Then run through the gears and reset the chain gap if necessary (it should be 6 mm away from all the sprockets).

11 The adjustment for SRAM shifters and gears can only be done at the lever. Stretch the cables to check they are bedded in, and re-adjust them if necessary. Run through the gears again and re-check the chain gap.

KNOW HOW

Tightening the gear inner cable

As with all gear mechanisms, you will need to pull up the slack as you tighten the gear inner cable. Unlike Shimano there are several options of SRAM shifter. In the instructions you will see that there are different fixing points for different gear setups and shifters.

Road gear systems

Mountain bike technology put the gear controls into the road rider's hands from the old position knee high on the down tube...

Rear mechs (derailleurs) and index systems

The rear mech is a sophisticated version of rather old fashioned technology, it carries the chain from sprocket to sprocket forming an external gear box running it slime and grit. And yet it works extremely well, as well as being light and cheap to produce.

The modern road rear mech gear has an index system. Shimano were the first company to successfully market one, the SIS (Shimano Index System). Usually, this is a seven-, eight-, nine- or 10-speed set-up.

A ratchet in the gear lever allows one gear or multiple gears to be shifted with very little effort. One click of the gear lever pulls the cables a preset amount, relative to the distance the mech has to move to hop the chain one sprocket on. This is very efficient, but relies on the cables staying put. In time, the cable will stretch and this slight movement throws the whole system out of whack.

Shimano STI (Shimano Total Integration) units

Shimano adopted an external cable system with the outer cables entering the levers at the top of the lever hoods. The brake cables pass under the bar tape. Shimano hoods are larger than Campagnolo and SRAM, and the whole brake lever moves in order to change gears.

Campagnolo Ergopower

The obvious difference from Shimano controls is that Ergopower brake and gear cables are both taped under the handlebar tape. The main difference in function is that the brake lever is independent from the gear levers and the downshift is facilitated with a thumb button on the inside of the lever hood. Campagnolo also developed their own take on index technology, and their Ergopower system was the first to have 10 gears.

SRAM

A late arrival to the road bike gear market, although SRAM already have a formidable reputation in the mountain bike market. Like Campagnolo, SRAM levers have an independent gear-shifting lever from the brake levers. Called Double Tap, their gearshift is done with just one lever: 'push' to shift up and 'tap' to shift down.

Background

Down-tube shifters were once the only gear-shifting choice. Nowadays they're rarely used – some climbers swap the front-mech shifter for a down-tube lever to save a few ounces, but the weight saved isn't really worth the effort. Down-tube levers mean that you have to take your hands off the handlebars to shift, but there's less cable and friction in the system, so they do last and provide very crisp shifts.

CHANGE & UPGRADE
Road-type gear cables
Nowhere are sweet changing gears more important than on a road bike built for speed...

Replacing inner cables

Gear cables have a smaller nipple than brake cables and they're thinner (1.2mm). Shimano gear cables have a slightly bigger nipple than Campagnolo cables, so they're incompatible across systems. A squirt of Teflon lube on the cable is a good idea before installation, as it'll keep the cables loose and free-running. through the lever mechanism, place the gear-shifter in the highest gear position. All systems require the lever and mech to be in top gear, so that the cable is slack and the nipple can be pushed out of the lever.

Gear & brake cables

What's the difference between them? Apart from size the important difference is the outer sleeve. The original sleeve was a tight spiral of steel wire usually covered with plastic. The brake cable is still like that. But the invention of index shifting required greater precision in the gear cable. A new 'compressionless' housing using a bundle of parallel wires, running more-or-less parallel to the cable was adopted. Don't use them for braking they'd collapse.

Gear-adjusters are attached to most older frames via a brazed on boss.

Campagnolo gear-adjusters rely on knurled-threaded adjusters with a spring under them to hold them in place – these do require cleaning and lubricating with a light oil to keep them easy to adjust.

Shimano adjusters have a lever that can be turned to micro-adjust the gears as you ride. Seeing as most frames come without the standard-type bosses, these adjusters are becoming rare.

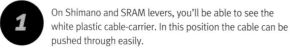

1 On Shimano and SRAM levers, you'll be able to see the white plastic cable-carrier. In this position the cable can be pushed through easily.

2 On Shimano levers, the cable simply passes straight through the lever and out of the cable port on the other side.

3 SRAM shifter cables are inserted at the inside, near the bottom of the lever-housing, and exit the lever at the top.

4 On SRAM levers, as with Campagnolo, the outer cable can be taped and fitted into the handlebar before the tape is applied.

5 New Campagnolo cables have a sharp, pointed end that makes threading the cable through the lever very easy.

6 Pull the cable through until the nipple seats itself in the cable-carrier.

CHANGE & UPGRADE
Installing a typical road-type rear mech

Three main systems dominate road bikes but the similarities make the mechanic's life relatively simple...

1 The rear mech needs to be installed onto the gear hanger. Check that the hanger is straight and that the threads are clean and uncrossed. If the hanger is bent or the mech cage is twisted, the system won't work. Use some grease or Ti-Prep lube on the threads to prevent the bolt from seizing.

2 The inner wire is clamped onto the rear mech by a washer. To see how this works, look for a channel moulded onto the body of the mech – the washer will be marked where the cable has been.

3 Screw the gear barrel-adjuster fully in, so that there will be plenty of adjustment available when setting the cable tension. If all the cable outer sections are properly inserted and the gear-shifter is in the highest gear position, it should be possible to pull the cable tight enough with your hand. Pull the cable in the direction of the channel identified in step 2. Lock it off with the retaining screw.

4 The main difference between Campagnolo, Shimano and SRAM rear mechs is that they use a different sprung-pivot fixing bolt. This is at the bolt and gives you the advantage of a mechanism that moves as you shift between the chainrings.

Retracing your steps

There are few things more frustrating and time wasting than taking a simple assembly apart, jockey wheels are a good example, and then finding you can't see how they go together again. Now almost everyone has a camera in their pocket, why not record your steps so you can retrace them easily?

5 Rear mechs work best with free-running jockey wheels. These can be replaced when the plastic wheels wear out. This improves shifting and helps keep the chain in contact with the sprockets on the cassette. To replace the jockey wheels, remove the pivot screws, paying attention to how it goes back together.

6 Strip and rebuild the jockey wheels after long periods of wet weather. The top jockey wheel may have a sealed bearing in it. It's worth stripping and reassembling both wheels. Clean them completely and reassemble using a Teflon lubricant.

7 Make sure that the jockey wheel is replaced so that it rotates in the right direction. There's usually an arrow on the plastic part of the wheel to help you do this. Once you've reassembled the cage, check that the top and bottom fixing-screws are tight.

8 Lubricate the parallelogram mechanism with a light Teflon-based lube, especially the pivot points and internal springs.

9 Adjust the limit screw marked 'H' when the chain is in the smallest sprocket (highest gear). It's important that the chain can run smoothly over the sprocket and can't move any further down the block, trapping the chain between frame and cassette. It's a good idea to fit the chain now.

10 Next, adjust the limit screw marked 'L' when the gear is in the largest sprocket. Double-check that the chain can reach this sprocket, and also that the chain can't jump over the top of the cassette and into the wheel. Also check that the mech can't hit the spokes of the wheel.

KNOW HOW

Indexing

1: Mountain bike and road indexing is much the same. To recap, you need to get the back wheel off the ground to leave your hands free. A workstand is ideal or you can suspend the bike from the ceiling.

2: Change up the gears one by one, starting at the smallest sprocket. Listen for noise as you change. Note how easily the chain skips the gears – if it struggles to make the next sprocket the cable is too loose, tighten it by screwing the barrel adjuster anti-clockwise. Now change back down the gears checking for delay or stickiness in the shift. If there is the cable is too tight. Loosen it by turning the adjuster clockwise. When the gears work well, tighten everything up, grab the cable in the centre of the top tube and pull it firmly away to stretch it and bed everything in. Make a final adjustment if needed and you're done.

EDITOR'S TIP If you have trouble remembering which is the low gear on the cassette, it may help that Low and Large begin with the same letter. Your lowest gear uses your largest rear sprocket.

CHANGE & UPGRADE
Cassettes and gear ratios

The mechanical advantage you get from gears depends on the number of teeth on the driving ring and the driven ring, something you can control...

The back wheel of your bicycle is powered through one of nine or 10 sprockets fixed by keyways to the rear freewheel hub. They come in groups called cassettes, which are put together with spacers and built with ramps to make it easier for the chain to go from one to the other.

Like everything else in the drivetrain, sprockets wear out and have to be changed for that reason. But the number of teeth on the rings you use alters the characteristics of your ride and you will find it useful to swap between groupings suitable on average terrain and those suitable for the mountains as required. The sort of choice and ease of use available today would have delighted the racers of old.

A 10-speed racer was once the pinnacle of bicycle technology. Index systems and the improvements made to hubs and mechs (derailleurs) has meant that larger gear ratios and wider spreads of gears are easily available.

Nowadays, most new bikes come with nine- or 10-speed cassettes and two or three chainwheels to provide anything from 18 to 30 gear ratios. Cassettes and chains are designed to work smoothly and shift crisply, which means that they're complicated and finely engineered, and therefore susceptible to wear and tear.

Changing cassettes is necessary for changes in terrain and types of riding (racing, training, touring, etc.) and although a cassette will last for a season or so (if you keep replacing the chain), it will wear out in the end.

Tools:
- chain whip
- cassette lock ring tool and spanner/wrench
- torque wrench

Cassette service and replacement
The Freehub body

All cassette configurations fit a freehub body that is attached to the rear hub. These have a set of shaped keyways and slots that allow the cassette sprockets to engage the hub. This also orientates the sprockets as the teeth have one way to face and a sequence of ramps and cut-aways to ensure smooth shifting.

Removing Cassettes (Campagnolo and Shimano)

1 Cassette servicing is best done with the wheel intact and the tyres still attached to the rim (in case you have to rest the wheel on the floor or lean on it for extra purchase).

2 The cassette lock-ring tool fits into the serrated inside of the lock-ring. Shimano and Campagnolo use the same principle, but not the same tool!

3 The standard socket-type tool can be held in place with the QR skewer to prevent it from rounding off the cassette lock-ring or slipping and causing injury or damage.

4 This double-sided tool also features a central locating pin (it's a personal favourite of mine!). It means you can use it with either system, and the pin helps hold the tool in place and allows for a firmer grip.

5 Remove the cassette using a chain whip and cassette lock-ring removal tool. The chain whip prevents the cassette from turning, and should be positioned so that the chain on the tool can wrap around the sprocket enough to prevent it from spinning when you push on the wrench.

6 Campagnolo 10-speed requires a chain whip with a 10-speed chain end to prevent damage to the sprockets and slipping as you apply pressure.

7 Stand over the wheel with the cassette facing away from you. Hold the chain whip in your left hand and the lock-ring tool in your right. Set the whip over the second biggest gear and position the tools as shown. Pushing down with both hands will undo the lock-ring.

8 The first two or three cassette sprockets will be loose, so be careful not to drop them. Lay the wheel flat on the workbench and take the sprockets off one by one, placing them down in the order in which they came off the wheel.

Shimano nine-speed and 10-speed set-ups

1 Apply a thin layer of grease or anti-seize to the cassette body before you slide the cassette back into place. This will prevent the cassette body from rusting. If there's any corrosion on the body, use a brass suede-shoe brush to clean it off.

2 The lock-ring threads into the cassette body and secures the sprockets. Because the cassette is integral to the drive, this needs to be tight.

3 Spacers may be required on some wheelsets, especially when they're not Shimano. Bear this in mind if you're setting up the gears too, as it can change the spacing and therefore the indexing for the rear mech.

4 Better-quality Shimano cassettes have the first few large cassette sprockets attached to a 'spider' or aluminium carrier to save some weight without losing rigidity.

5 The remaining cassette sprockets are loose and have a spacer (marked nine- or 10-speed) to ensure the correct spacing and alignment of the sprockets.

6 The serrated teeth pressed into the last sprocket and the underside of the lock-ring prevent it from vibrating loose.

Sprockets: Campagnolo 10-speed hubs

1 Like Shimano, Campagnolo has a special cassette body that orientates the cassette sprockets. They also come in a variety of materials and qualities.

2 Between the first and second cluster of sprockets, Campagnolo use a wider spacer that also has a larger outside diameter.

3 The second pair of sprockets are also held on a carrier – in Record, these first two clusters are made from titanium.

4 When the first four gears are in place, there's another special wider-diameter spacer to put in place before the smaller single loose sprockets can be added.

5 Like Shimano, the smaller set of sprockets will have single spacers between each one.

6 The final two sprockets may not require the spacers, as they're ready-machined with the spacer attached, and the last sprocket will have serrations on the outside to keep it tight up against the lock-ring.

Sprockets: Campagnolo nine-speed hubs

The better-quality nine-speed units are the same as 10-speed to install, although the cheaper-quality cassettes can have simple plastic spacers and are less complicated to install. However, they both fit the same Campagnolo nine-ten speed pattern hubs.

All systems

Once the cassette system is in place, tighten the lock-ring to 35–50Nm. You'll be surprised how tight this is, but the cassette bears a considerable load and needs to be checked for tightness regularly.

Cassette tips

Although SRAM cassette sprockets do work with Shimano hubs (and vice versa), they won't fit on new Dura Ace cassette bodies and will only fit older Shimano hubs.

Cassette carriers come with SRAM, Miche and Campagnolo cassettes – these are plastic clips that line up with the cassette body's grooves. These will allow you to simply slide the sprockets into place without having to replace each one individually, which will prevent you from missing out spacers or dropping them all on the floor.

Cassette and chainset configurations

A vast range of ratios is possible using custom components but these have stood the test of time...

Standard cassette ratios

11–21 A racing ratio for mainly flat courses, time trials and for sprinter-roadmen, this is not a cassette ratio for hilly rides or long training weekends in the Alps. Usually used by specialists with standard 53/39 chainsets for racing only.

11–23 or 12–23 A good, all-round racing ratio, suitable for quick, slightly hilly circuits. This is the standard road riding/racing ratio and can be used with either standard or Compact chainsets.

12–25 Better suited to hillier circuits. This is the ratio that most professional riders use in the Alps and Pyrenees during the Tour de France (though usually with a 39-tooth inner chainring!). For we lesser mortals with less painful ambitions, this also combines very well with Compact ratios.

13–29 The choice ratio for riding in the high mountains Works best with Compact (I like the 50/36 crank here) and it gives almost as many options as a triple chainset.

Variable gearing allows you to vary the number of times your back wheel goes around each time your legs turn the chainset one full turn. The teeth of the rings and sprockets all being the same size a chainset of 50 teeth, for example, will turn a sprocket of ten teeth and the wheel attached to it five times for every revolution (which makes quite a hard gear to push and propels the bike pretty fast). Cyclists call it a big or tall gear. On the other hand, a 30

on the front driving a 27 on the back is almost one for one and could inch you up a mountain at snail's pace if you can contrive to maintain traction. Cyclists are obsessed by gears and like to add to the confusion by expressing them in inches, the inches being the diameter of penny-farthing wheel you would need to have to obtain the same gear. Fun but not need-to-know stuff. However, you do need to know which gear ratios best suit the sort of riding you want to do...

Standard Chainset configurations

Hill climbing ratios v weight is the debate here. Do you need a triple chainring or will a compact do as well?

Standard double:

52/42 or 53/39

The averagely fit rider wants to make sure the power will always be on – and a 53/12 is big enough to keep it pushing down all but the steepest hills. The 39 will give some respite in the hills although not enough, perhaps, for the rider who's more interested in training than comfort.

Compact double:

48/36; 50/36; 50/34

If it's all about comfort and having enough gears for the hills, the compact drive allows you to retain those clean road bike lines without adding extra weight. How often do you actually use a 53/12 anyway, aficionados will ask.

Triple chain ring:

52/42/30

One for the practical cyclist who wants all the ratios right there and doesn't bother too much about the extra maintenance and weight.

Off the shelf ratios

- Campagnolo 10-speed cassettes usually come in the following ratios: 11–21; 11–23; 11–25; 12–23; 12–25; 13–26; 13–29.
- Campagnolo nine-speed cassettes are now less common, but usually come in: 12–23; 13–23; 13–26.
- Shimano nine- and 10-speed cassettes are usually available in: 11–21; 11–23; 12–21; 12–23; 12–25; 12–27.

Mavic

Mavic's own system is slightly different again – their M10 cassette can be used in a variety of combinations, as each cog is individually mounted. It's totally customised and supplied with nine- and 10-speed spacer kits for use with either Campagnolo gear system.

5

Wheels and Tyres

Without which there would be no bicycle

The spoked wheel is miracle of lightweight strength and rigidity, robust enough to support the chain driven gear system that had its beginnings in the late 19th century with the safety bicycle. And the pneumatic tyre, invented by Dunlop in 1888, made the whole safety bicycle experiment a viable and reasonably comfortable experience for all, men and women alike.

It's hard for us to realise the impact that the bicycle made at start of the 20th Century as less affluent men and women found a relatively affordable way to explore the countryside under their own steam. We can get some idea, perhaps, from the explosion of mountain biking in the 80s, when a sport which had been sadly crushed by traffic and the car, blossomed again off

"The bicycle has been a potent agent of social change three times in 100 years"

the road away from the cops, the cars and the concrete. The bicycle has been a potent agent of social change perhaps three times in 100 years and who would bet that its electric-assisted mode will not make an even bigger impact in the energy-conscious 21st Century?

The quick release

Of all the ways wheels are attached to bikes this is the most useful and most often misused

The quick-release lever (or QR) was invented by the Italian engineer and racer Tuilio Campagnolo. In the days when he was racing, the riders had to stop to change gear on their fixed-wheel bikes, swapping the wheel around for the other side of the hub where a lower gear sprocket was fitted. One cold day on the Croce d'Aune, with his hands freezing, he couldn't undo the wing nuts that held his wheel in place – legend has it that he invented the quick-release lever as a result of this hardship. These days, the standard road-bike wheel has a QR mechanism which is essentially the same design as the

one Mr Campagnolo invented. This system is excellent for removing the wheels instantly, which is great for repairing punctures, quick racing-wheel changes, or putting your bike in the back of your car.

But, to the uninitiated, a QR mechanism can be potentially hazardous if done up incorrectly. On most bikes the front-wheel system has a slightly different technique from the rear-wheel system. If you're removing both wheels, take the front one out first – this will make the bike easier to manage and means that you won't have to drag the chain and gears on the ground.

Off-road QRs

Mountain bikers with disc brakes should take special care to tighten the QR properly. Discs exert powerful stresses on the hub which can loosen an incorrectly installed QR. It has happened. 'Lawyer tabs' (see below) get their name from the early days when a few MTB companies were sued after front wheels fell out unexpectedly with catastrophic results.

Front wheels

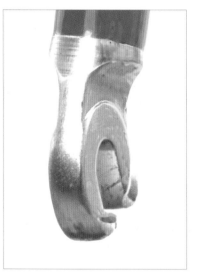

1 'Lawyer tabs' are designed to prevent the wheel from falling out should the QR lever be done up too loosely.

2 Once the QR is undone the wheel may still not drop out completely, so the nut on the non-lever side needs to be loosened a little more. The key here is to remember how much you've undone it and not to remove it completely. To clear the tabs, undo the nut – three full turns will be enough on most bikes. The wheel will then drop out.

3 The springs on the inside of the QR mechanism help centralise the nut and the lever to push them away from the bike. They also make it easier to replace the wheel, as you don't have to centre the assembly. This leaves your hands free to hold the bike and position the wheel into the fork ends.

4 The front wheel has to be firmly placed into the dropouts before you can do up the lever. For this reason I suggest you replace the wheels with the bike on the ground – this way the weight of the bike can help make the wheels go in straight. It's best to do the levers up when the weight of the bike is on the wheels. You can lean over and do the front wheel up this way.

Rear Wheels

5 The chain should be on the smallest sprocket/cog and the largest chainring, so change into this gear before you start. This makes it easier to get the chain off the cassette and easier to replace the wheel afterwards.

6 Stand behind the bike and hold the bike upright with your legs trapping the wheel, leaving your hands free to remove the wheel. Now undo the lever.

Tightening the QR

Tightening the QR adequately is essential for safety and this needs to be checked regularly, especially before and after rides. Also, be careful where you position the lever in the closed position. Place the front QR so that it runs behind the fork, and the rear one in line with the seat stay (pointing towards the saddle). This will also make it easier to undo the lever in a hurry.

7 The wheel remains trapped into the bike by the chain, so twist the mech backwards to release it. The chain should stay on the front chainwheel, so start with the chain in this position when replacing the wheel.

8 To replace the rear wheel, the mech needs to be sprung into the correct position with the wheel in the bike. Next, wrap the chain over the top of the smallest sprocket to help the wheel slot into the dropouts.

9 Pull the wheel upwards and backwards, and it should slot into place easily. If it doesn't, the wheel may have become snagged on the brake pads, or the mech may not be in the correct gear position.

10 Don't adjust the nut on the QR lever, as the rear wheel should clear the dropouts and slip in easily. However, it's worth checking that the lever feels tight as it closes. Rest your weight on the bike, as this will keep the wheel central.

11 Once the wheel is slotted into the dropouts, slowly tighten the nut up until the lever starts to tighten. When the lever is firm directly in line with the skewer it will close tightly enough.

12 It should close firmly, needing enough effort so that you have to use your thumb and press hard. Any harder and you'll struggle to undo it again. Check that the wheel spins centrally and you're safe to ride.

REPAIR & MAINTENANCE
How to deal with a puncture on the trail

Punctures are a fact of cycling life. The tubeless tyres filled with sealant, now found on many mountain bikes and soon to be seen more on the road, certainly help as does strategically placed Kevlar, but for all our tricks flats will always be with us.

For that reason, most seasoned riders carry a supply of inner tubes so they can get up and going quickly and repair the old tube later at home. Standing beside a busy road or crouching in the rain in some forest, these are no places to be juggling with glue and chalk. You can replace a tube quite quickly with practise, but it's worth taking your time so you discover the cause of the damage and avoid flatting another tube and make sure you get the tyre properly up to pressure. Here's how it's done in ten easy steps. Don't be put off that we're using a mountain bike tyre as an example, standard tyres work just about the same.

Tools:
- tyre levers
- spare tube (or puncture kit)
- mini-pump

1 As soon as you realise you have a flat, stop. It's better to get on with fixing the flat than trying to ride any further on a potentially hazardous wheel. Riding with a flat can also damage the rim should you hit anything hard on the trail. Stopping straight away may also allow you to find the hole in the tyre and remove any sharp objects that may have become trapped in the tread. Remove the wheel and hang your bike up on a suitable hedge or tree branch. If the puncture is in the rear wheel, try not to dangle the chain in the mud.

2 Mountain bike tyres won't usually need two tyre levers as shown here, but road tyres may. Push the tyre away to reveal the bead, slip the lever tip under the bead and simply pull the bead off. If you have to use two levers, pull one section off first and then move a little further around the rim. The second lever will be harder to pull, but should pop the tyre off easily. Run the lever around the rim, removing one side of the tyre from the rim. Do not remove the tyre completely yet.

3 Pull the tube away from the tyre and pack it away – you can fix it later. Check that there is nothing wrong with the rim tape beneath the tube, as it can sometimes come loose under the tyre and move, exposing a spoke hole that can pinch the tube.

4 Double-check the tyre walls for thorns and anything that may have penetrated the tyre. If there is a large gash in the sidewall you may have to use a tyre patch; you can improvise by using a piece of cardboard, but the best option is a patch that can be stuck to the inside of the tyre. This is just a temporary fix until you can get a new tyre.

Top tyre tips

- Swap the front tyre with the back tyre on a regular basis. This will help your tyres last longer, as the rear tyre wears faster than the front.
- New tyres can have a residue on them that can make them a bit slippery. A (careful) wet ride and a proper wash with degreaser will remove this pretty quickly.
- Place a new inner tube in a plastic bag with a sprinkling of talc and give it a shake – this will coat the tube and help it slip into place under the tyre.

5 Slightly inflate the replacement tube with two strokes of a mini-pump, just enough for the tube to take shape. Next, insert the valve into the valve hole. Ensure that the valve is seated properly into the rim, then push the tyre over the top of the tube.

6 Work the tube into the carcass of the tyre – inflating it slightly. Beware of folds in the tube at this point and do not twist the tube as you return it to the tyre, as this can pinch and even puncture once the tyre is re-inflated, or make it inflate unevenly.

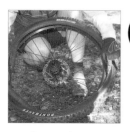

7 You should tuck the tube so it sits inside the tyre carcass but, more importantly, away from the rim. Leaving any part of the tube outside the tyre makes it very difficult to replace the tyre without pinching the tube.

8 Now, start to return the tyre bead into the rim. Start opposite the valve hole and work the tyre either side with two hands, until there is only a small amount left. If the last part of the tyre can be pulled onto the rim by hand, that is the safest way.

9 Once the tyre is back on the rim, check that the bead hasn't snagged the tube, or that part of the tube isn't trapped between the bead and the rim. This can push the tyre off the rim or make it roll unevenly, or even explode once the tyre has been pumped up to a decent pressure.

10 Finally, pump the tyre up to the recommended pressure. If the tyre wobbles as you spin the wheel, re-seat it by letting most of the air out and pulling the tyre away from the bead. This will help the bead sit into the rim.

FAQ: *Is it true you get more punctures in the wet or does it just seem like that?*

It's true. The water lubricates the rubber and makes it easier for a spike to penetrate.

REPAIR & MAINTENANCE
Replacing spokes

You can replace a spoke easily enough, but the breakage may be a sign that the wheel is getting old and it's time to have it rebuilt

Replacing a spoke is a straightforward operation, but it can be time consuming. Spokes will give little warning before they snap, and the usual causes are previous damage or uneven spoke tension due to rim damage or repeated heavy impacts.

Since spokes tend to break as a wheel is reaching the end of its serviceable life, it's worth considering a re-build after you break one. Repeated spoke failure (where you have broken several spokes one after the other) usually means that the rim is wrecked and the spokes are struggling to support it. Properly built wheels from a good wheel builder will not break spokes, unless the spokes are damaged somehow. Properly tensioned hand-built wheels are less likely to fail and they are a wise investment. Broken spokes usually occur on the drive side of the rear wheel. With singlespeed wheels and 150 mm rear axles, broken

Tools:
- spoke key
- spare spokes (make sure you have the correct length)
- screwdriver and/or nipple driver

spokes are becoming less common as there is less dish in the rear wheel and therefore the spokes are under less strain on the drive side.

1 In emergencies, you can replace the spoke with the tyre in place, if you have one the right length. It's always best to remove the tyre, tube and rim tape so that you can access the nipple and replace it if necessary. Over-long spokes will protrude into the rim cavity and burst the tube so be precise.

2 If the spoke is outbound (the head of the spoke faces into the hub centre) you will have to thread the spoke in from the opposite side of the wheel. This is the easiest way to lace the spoke into the wheel.

3 The spoke can pass through the lower part of the spokes on the opposite side of the wheel. The spoke will then usually travel over the first two crossing spokes and under the last one before reaching the rim.

4 Inbound spokes (where the head of the spoke faces out from the hub centre) are far more tricky to lace. You have to angle the spoke upwards so that it avoids the crossing at the other side of the wheel. Be careful not to bend the spoke too much as this will weaken it.

5 Spokes cross three times between the hub and the rim. Depending on the way the wheel has been laced, the spokes will cross under twice and over once or over twice and under once. Either way, it is essential that you copy this lacing when you replace a spoke to maintain the integrity and strength of the wheel.

6 In order to lace the spoke around the rim, you will have to push it under the rim. Protect the rim from being scratched by the threads when you do this by placing a finger or thumb over the end of the spoke, at the same time bending the spoke very gently and evenly so that it can tuck under the rim.

7 In this photograph the replacement spoke is positioned behind the final crossing spoke and is long enough to insert into the rim cavity through the eyelet.

8 The correct length spoke will meet the rim eyelet and should be long enough to pass through the nipple and be level with the top of it on the inside of the rim. Any longer and the spoke will be too slack on the nipple. The nipple can be replaced if necessary; nipples can round off with poorly fitting spoke keys and poor quality nipples can shear off.

9 Take up the slack with a screwdriver before you start to true the wheel. Make a note of how far the other spokes protrude from the nipple and – if you have the correct length spoke – you can get the spoke to a similar position.

10 Eyeletted rims last longer than non-eyeletted ones and experience fewer breakages as the eyelets allow the nipples to move slightly inside the rim. The eyelets also reinforce the rim and are easier to true as the nipples move freely inside them.

KNOW HOW

Broken spokes

A common reason for a broken spoke is the derailleur over shifting into the wheel from lowest gear. Contact like this can damage spokes and cause them to break at a later date. At worst it can ruin the wheel and/or rip the rear mech off. So adjust the mech using the limit screws if it makes the slightest contact.

EDITOR'S TIP

"Always have another wheel handy so you can copy the spoke pattern, especially if you are replacing more than one spoke."

REPAIR & MAINTENANCE
Truing wheels

From bitter experience we advise that you should think very carefully before trying to true wheels yourself, but you ought to know what it's all about...

Much as I love wheel building, this is not the place to show you how to do it. Gerd Schraener's *The Art of Wheelbuilding* and Jobst Brandt's *The Bicycle Wheel* both offer excellent tuition and guidance in this very technical process. Here I will show you the basics of wheel truing and hope you'll get the bug and want to learn more about how wheels are built.

First, assess the wheel and decide where the imbalance could be. Spin the wheel and see where the buckles are and where the wheel has uneven tension. A wheel is like a suspension bridge and any imbalance in the supports (spokes) places more stress on the neighbouring supports. The most common problem is a broken spoke, but spokes can also be loose or damaged, which will also cause a wobble.

When you spin the wheel, it should sit centrally in the jig (or bike if you are on the trail), so your job is to find out where, and more importantly how, the wheel is being pulled away from this centre line. Do not attempt to true a wheel until you have a good idea what is causing the buckle.

Lateral (side to side) buckles are the easiest to solve:
- if the wheel hops to the left, tighten the spoke on the right or loosen the spoke on the left;
- if the wheel hops to the right, tighten the spoke on the left or loosen the spoke on the right.

However, radial (up and down) buckles are different:
- if the hop is towards the hub, the spoke is too tight;
- if the hop is away from the hub, the spoke is too loose.

Tools:
- pointed bradawl or small screwdriver
- truing stand
- spoke keys (there are a variety of nipple sizes depending on spoke type and gauge)
- dishing stick
- spoke tension meter (optional)

So, if the rim hops to the left and towards the hub at the same time, there is a spoke pulling too tightly on the left, and if the rim hops to the right and away from the hub at the same time, there is a loose spoke on the right.

That is the simple version; the rest is about practice and experience – just like tuning a piano, apparently. The first few times you true a wheel will take you some time, but if you can be patient (and practise) it will come as second nature. Remember to make small adjustments at first and mark the rim with chalk or wrap a strip of tape on the suspect spokes so that you always know where you started.

Rear wheels have tighter spokes on the drive side than they do on the non-drive side. The non-drive spokes are also longer. This means that they require fewer turns than the drive side; it depends on the wheel but the ratio is about 2:1. On front hubs you will always need to loosen or tighten the same amount on both sides. Whatever you do, do it gradually and no more than a quarter turn at a time.

FAQ: *Is it true that a spoke key can do more damage to a bicycle than a lump hammer?*

No, but this old bicycle mechanic's joke points out the dangers of impatient and ham-fisted wheel tuning. The spoked wheel is strong and light when properly built and maintained. Abused it can quickly turn into a heap of scrap.

1 Treat the spokes in groups rather than individually. The usual cause of a buckle is a broken spoke; however, here we are trying to find the loose ones that may just require tightening. Grab several spokes at a time and squeeze them to feel where the problem is before you start to true the wheel.

2 Always use a spoke key that fits the nipples snugly. A loose-fitting key will ruin the nipple very easily, especially if the nipple is tight. If the spoke becomes very tight and the rim still needs to move some more, you may have to loosen the opposite spoke to allow a little more movement. Spokes tighten with a standard right-hand thread, so if you are using your right hand you will need to turn the spoke key towards you to tighten the spoke and away from you to loosen it.

3 A severe radial hop or a skip in the rim can signify a set or group of very loose or tight spokes. As with the lateral truing, you need careful judgement to decide which spokes to tackle first. Grab hold of a few and try to find the loose ones first. Then, using quarter-turns only, adjust the tension in two or four spokes at a time – you need to pull on both sides equally to prevent the wheel going out laterally as well as radially.

4 'Dish' describes the shape of the wheel. Basically, the hub lock nuts (where the wheel is held in the frame or forks) and the rim need to sit in line for the bike to handle properly. Wheel dish is determined by measuring the wheel with a dishing stick, which checks that the lock nuts are equally spaced on either side of the rim. Dish guarantees that the wheels will run in line and also allows for efficient braking. Disc brakes take up space on the non-drive side of the wheel, but this can reduce the dish and therefore create more equal tension in the wheel, which is a good thing.

5 Rim dents and wear to the braking surfaces will make a difference to the tension in the wheel. Dents usually happen when the wheel pinch punctures due to hitting a root or a rock. Mountain bike wheels will absorb a lot of shock and the rims are made from very strong heat-treated alloys, so the chances are the rim will dent rather than collapse.

6 Accurate truing has to be done using a quality wheel jig rather than with the wheel still in the bike. Wheel jigs provide more stability, so the wheel doesn't rock around when you spin it. The wheel jig pictured here has self-centring jaws and retaining arms so that the rim will be perfect if it is trued to the guides. The jaws can be adjusted so that the rim drags on them to give you a visual and audible clue as to where the buckle is.

7 Professional wheel builders will use a DT spoke tension meter. This can accurately measure spoke tension and enables a good wheel builder to keep variation in spoke tension to around 10 per cent. This is also useful when truing a wheel, as you can assess which spokes are being pushed too hard and are therefore likely to break first.

8 Once you are happy that the wheel is round again, 'stress' the wheel in your lap or gently on the floor. Do not stress the wheel with your full weight, especially if the bearings are sealed as they are vulnerable to side loads. You will hear the wheel click and ping as the spokes 'find' their position. This may mean that the rim moves a little, so double-check it in the jig before you're finished.

9 Finally, replace the rim tape. I always use tape that will stick to the rim; this way you know it will not come loose and move around under the tube. Plastic tape is better than cloth as cloth tape holds water and will rust the eyelets, which in turn can seize the nipples. Rim tape should be renewed every time it is removed – never re-use old tape.

UPGRADE...
Carbon Seatpost
A good place to start when reducing bike weight is to fit a quality carbon seatpost; it can also achieve greater comfort by reducing road buzz.

DANGER!

Most rims designed for use with rim brakes have a wear indicator, which is either a black line or a series of dots on the middle of the rim. As the rim wears, these marks slowly disappear and when you can't see them any more the rim needs changing. It is important to keep an eye on this as rims can wear severely and the bead on the rim will eventually fail, leading to a very nasty accident.

CHANGE & UPGRADE
Cup-and-cone style wheel hubs

Wheel bearings take a hammering on a bike. Are you up to stripping them or should you buy spare wheels and let the bike shop take the strain? Here's how it's done so you can decide...

Cup-and-cone hubs with loose bearings are very simple to service. The first few times it can be challenging, but experience really speeds the process up. The key is to make sure that all the components are in top condition – any wear and tear to the cones or bearings means that the parts should be replaced.

Most Shimano road hubs, from Tiagra to Dura Ace use the same principle and many older Campagnolo hubs also follow the same pattern. Most contemporary Campagnolo hubs from Mirage to Record have an oversized aluminium axle and system that requires no specialist cone spanners or tools – they have several specific parts but are simple to adjust, and everything is replaceable and serviceable.

Hubs will need a complete service every four to six months, depending on weather conditions and how often you ride. Fresh grease and regular adjustment will keep hubs rolling for a long time. Shimano cone hubs are excellent because you can rebuild them very easily and quickly, and they use top-quality bearings and hardened steel cones. Look after them properly and

Tools:
- pointed bradawl or small screwdriver
- 2 x 13mm cone spanners (Shimano use 13mm cones, but they can vary in size)
- torque wrench
- 17mm open-ended spanner (or cone spanner)
- grease
- axle vice and bench-mounted vice
- 10mm Allen key

they'll easily outlast the spokes and the rims. However, loose hubs don't last very long. Grab your wheel by the tyre and shake the wheel from side to side while it's still in the bike. If you feel a slight knock or 'play' through the tyre, the hub is loose. This means that the bearings are bashing around inside the hub and slowly disintegrating, and the seals are more exposed, allowing water and muck into the hub. Leave the hub like this and it won't take long for the internals to fail completely. Rebuilding the wheel with a new hub is far more costly and time-consuming than replacing the grease and the bearings every few months.

The right stuff

Using the right grease is important. Use a specially formulated synthetic bicycle grease that's waterproof and of a consistent quality – specialist bike lubricant manufacturers have what you need. However, make sure you don't overdo it – too much grease can make bearings drag, and already difficult adjustments become harder still.

 The key to easy hub servicing is only working on one side. If you keep one side intact, the factory setting spacing over the lock nuts is easier to retain. All front hubs measure 100mm over the lock nuts – this measurement is critical so that the wheel can easily be replaced in the forks.

 Undo and remove the lock nut, the washer and, finally, the cone. Cone spanners are very thin and flat. This means that they can fit into the machined flats on the sides of the cone and can adjust and tighten the cones without snagging on the washer and lock nut. Use the correct size (and don't use cone spanners to remove your pedals, as this will damage them!). Hold the cone with a cone spanner and release the lock nut with a 17mm spanner.

 The cone is made from hardened steel and has a highly polished bearing surface. Inspect the cone carefully for any rough patches on the surface, which is known as pitting. On most front wheels there's only a cone, washer and lock nut.

 Remove the cone, spacers and – very carefully – the axle. Place the threaded components down on the workbench in the order they came off the hub to help you remember the order to return them in. Clean the axle and cones, leaving one side on the axle and in one piece.

Keep all the old bearings so that you can check you're replacing the same size and quantity. It's good practice to replace the bearings after every strip-down. The bearings are slightly more vulnerable than the cones and the hub surfaces, so they tend to wear out first. Look at them closely and you'll see tiny potholes. Bearings need to be mirror-finished, so if they're even slightly dull they need replacing. It's useful to have a magnetic screwdriver for this job, as it'll make re-installation far easier. Store spare bearings on a magnet to make them easier to manage.

Clean the inside of the bearing surfaces and inspect for damage. If the bearing surfaces and cones are pitted, you'll need to replace either the cones or the hub assembly. Replacing the cones and the bearings and resetting them in grease will usually solve any hub roughness.

7 To grease the hub cups properly, you don't have to remove the hub seals – they're factory-fitted and are very hard to replace, as they're pressed into the shell of the hub, and it's possible to see into the hub with the seals in place. However, if you do have to remove them, be very careful. Wrap a rag around a tyre lever and prise the seals out carefully. Don't use a screwdriver as this can bend the seal, and if that happens you'll never get it back in again. To replace the seal, use your fingers to locate it and then tap it home using a rubber mallet.

8 When all the bearings are installed, take the loose cone and push it back into the hub. Rotate it a couple of times to seat the bearings. This will also tell you if there's any damage to the bearing surface inside the hub, and will stick the bearings in place so you can turn the wheel over to do the other side. Next, double-check that there are the right amount of bearings in the hub. Lastly, smear a little more grease on top of the bearings and check there isn't any grease inside the hub. You'll then be able to push the axle through without making a big mess.

9 Replace the axle (remember to return it the same way round it was at removal). As you've only disturbed one set of bearings, the spacing won't have been altered. Screw the cone onto the axle and up to the bearings.

10 Spin the axle in your fingers and 'rock' it slightly from side to side – you're looking for the point at which there's no 'play', only smooth spinning. When you're happy that the bearings are running smoothly, replace the washer and then the lock nut. At this stage they need to be finger-tight.

11 With practice, you'll be able to set the cones like this and simply do up the cone as in step 2. However, when tightening the lock nut for the last time, you may also either loosen the cone slightly or tighten it. To set the cones properly, you'll need two cone spanners to work against one another until the axle spins freely.

FAQ: *Is it true that ball bearings always roll under the fridge?*

Yes. Even if you don't have a fridge.

CHANGE & UPGRADE
Cartridge-style wheel hubs

Cartridge bearings are easier to deal with in many ways, here's what the job entails, illustrated on a back wheel hub this time...

The following method for fitting new bearings in hubs with cartridge units is fairly straightforward. Each manufacturer will have its own tools and bearings, but the principles remain very similar. Cartridge bearing hubs rely on a sealed-bearing cartridge unit that can be removed and replaced, whereas cup-and-cone systems rely on loose ball bearings and adjustable bearing surfaces.

With cartridge bearing hubs, the ball bearings are set into a hardened steel cartridge casing that press-fits into the hub shell or freewheel body. This unit is packed with grease and sealed with plastic or labyrinth seals. The quality is determined by the number of bearings and amount of grease packed into them.

Once the bearing is pushed into the hub, the axle is then press-fitted into the hole through the middle of the cartridge. All this has to be a precise and tight fit to support the wheel and to spin efficiently. The obvious advantage of sealed cartridge bearings like this is that they require less adjustment and servicing than standard cup-and-cone bearings. However, they're only as good as the quality of the bearings and standard of engineering of the hub shells. A cartridge hub at the cheaper end of the range may have push-fit covers and less sealing than a Shimano or Campagnolo cup-and-cone hub. So, shop wisely, as good-quality hubs can be built several times over into fresh rims, and last much longer than cheap ones. Sealed bearings don't like side loads and can easily be damaged, so treat them with care and always use the manufacturer's recommended tools.

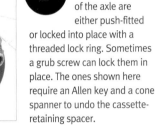

1 The spacers at the end of each side of the axle are either push-fitted or locked into place with a threaded lock ring. Sometimes a grub screw can lock them in place. The ones shown here require an Allen key and a cone spanner to undo the cassette-retaining spacer.

2 This non-drive-side spacer threads onto the axle end – most are a simple push-on fitting. The axle and the bearing take the strain, so oversize axles are a good idea with sealed bearings, as they fit better, can handle much more abuse and tend to twist less under drive. Power transfer to the rear wheel should be better and the bearings should last longer.

3 With the spacers and lock nuts removed, the cassette body can be taken off. On most cartridge hubs the cassette will be a push-fit secured by the drive-side spacer. However, some use a Shimano-type cassette freewheel body that's bolted to the hub body. You'll need a 10mm Allen key to remove this.

4 Push out the old cartridge bearings. This wheel's axle has to be tapped out with a plastic mallet. Once one side has been removed, the cartridge will pop out, still attached to the axle. The axle can then be used to tap out any bearings remaining in the hub shell.

5 This Bontrager hub has a bolt-on cassette body and is removed in the same way as a Shimano hub (see step 3) with a 10mm Allen key. You can see the collar that holds the cartridge bearing. This needs to be cleaned thoroughly before a new bearing can be installed.

6 The remaining bearing on the axle can be tapped off by placing the axle in a die. This allows you to use the axle as a drift to remove the remaining bearing on the other side of the hub. To replace the bearing you'll have to place it on top of the die and tap the axle back in. When it's flush to the shoulder in the centre of the axle, it's ready to be reinstalled on the hub.

7 The new bearings can be replaced. All sealed bearings have a code number and can be bought at most engineering suppliers or your local bike shop.

8 Use an appropriate die to seat the new bearings into the hub. They're a tight fit, but must be installed gently so as not to damage the bearing unit or the seals. Put some grease around the outside of the bearing and place it squarely onto the hub. Use an insertion tool that's the same size as the outer metal part of the bearing. Gently tap the bearing home with the plastic mallet.

Sealed bearings

Remove sealed bearings with an old axle or soft drift. Be careful not to damage the inside of the hub body – a light tap should be enough to free the cartridge. With care the seals can be removed with a scalpel blade and the old grease flushed out with a de-greaser. Use a grease gun to inject fresh grease into the bearings inside the collars.

"Avoid strong solvent-based lubricants on sealed bearing hubs, as they can damage the seals and flush out grease from the bearings."

9 Most cartridge bearing hubs have their own type of cassette which pulls off once the lock rings and spacers have been removed. Inside the hub is a series of teeth and on the cassette body are three sprung pawls. These pawls engage with the teeth when you pedal and 'click' around freely when you stop.

10 Here you can see the serrated part inside the hub. This needs to be completely cleaned out and lightly greased before you replace the rebuilt cassette body.

11 Carefully remove the pawls and clean all the dirty grease off the cassette body. Use a toothbrush to clean out all the pawl indentations and spring channels.

12 The cassette shown here has a single circular spring, so the pawls need to be set in grease and then have the spring replaced over them. This does take time, as it's quite fiddly. Many hubs have springs for individual pawls. If these fail they'll need replacing, as they can get stuck into the serrated parts and ruin the freewheel.

13 Use a lightweight grease on the freewheel pawls to avoid chain-sag. To replace the cassette body and fit it into the hub, you'll need to push the pawls into the body. Some hubs supply a ring clip tool for this. Once placed, double-check that the cassette body rotates freely before you rebuild the rest of the hub.

Tyre facts

Tyres were essential to the rise of the bicycle historically and still, today, our choice of tyre has more effect on the ride of our bicycles than most of us realise

Tyres have been central to the development of the bicycle. Without the invention of the pneumatic tyre in 1888 there would have been no cycling explosion in the 1890s, no Knickerbocker glory, no middle class experience of personal freedom and, to be a little fanciful, not much of a British motor industry when the time came.

Again it was the fat, low-pressure tyre, borrowed from the American balloon-tyred cruiser (probably one of the worst bikes ever produced) which made it possible to ride bikes in the mountains of Marin Country and hence off road all over the world. The tyres, 'fat' and 'knobbly' were what first separated the mountain bike, in the public's imagination, from the skinny tyres of the speed seeking road brigade.

All that was some time ago, and the recent development of new compounds has been an equally important advance. Certainly Steve Peat, 2009 World Downhill Champion and serial World Cup Champion puts the new sticky tyre compounds up there on a level with suspension as important advances in the improvement of downhill mountain bike racing. They can change the whole way you ride a bike.

Tubs and clinchers

The vast majority of bike tyres have a bead that runs around the edge and secures the tyre by locking under the lip of the rim. A steel bead keeps a circular shape, a Kevlar bead is lighter and flexible so can be folded. A traditional form of un-beaded tyre, which is growing more popular as carbon fibre becomes the material of choice for road bikes, is the tubular (tub) or sew up tyre. The edges of the tyre are sewn up around the tube and the whole thing cemented to the wheel so there's no need for fancy rim shapes, which are hard to make in carbon.

Compounds

The quality of the rubber in your tyre has a big effect on the grip you get and the speed with which it wears. Soft compounds grip more and wear faster. Using different compounds together is the trick. For example a dual compound tyre might have a hard strip down the centre for wear getting softer towards the edges for grip in corners.

Treads and volume

In the early days, mountain bike tyres were little more than mini tractor tyres, but today the combination of new compounds and cunning tread patterns have produced specifics for everything from desert sand to slushy snow. Choice is hard, you have your favourites and then you find another type that blows those away. See what the manufacturer of your sort of bike sends his upper mid-range bikes out with. A manufacturer wants his star mass-market machine to ride well.

With road tyres it comes down to fat or thin, width and height are more important than any sort of tread which is often more for inspiring confidence than usefulness. Fatter tyres cushion the ride and put more rubber on the road for grip, thin tyres transfer shock through your hands. Opinion is changing towards the idea that a properly inflated fatter tyre need not incur more rolling resistance than a skinny one, and it's probably best to go for comfort and ride quality first. A 700x23c tyre is a sound all round road tyre.

Pressure

There is nothing to be gained by over or under-inflating tyres. The suggested pressures have been well thought through, so stay in that general area. Higher pressure does no harm on hard dry terrain or to cut through the slush on muddy roads, and softer tyres put more rubber on the road for better grip at the risk of more punctures.

UPGRADE...
Brake Blocks
Good quality blocks offer greater performance, but choose the correct type of block for your rim of choice.

Universal standard tubeless tyres

The emergence and general acceptance of tubeless MTB tyres is one of the most significant developments of the last few years. The tyre is sealed to the rim and the spoke holes are configured in a double-walled rim, so that an airtight seal is possible.

This means you can do away with the weak link, the inner tube. Tubeless tyres are very popular with racers as they only fail if the tyre gashes very badly. The technology will get better and should make punctures a thing of the past.

The development of a similar system for road tyres has been slow to catch on due, partly, to resistance from pros who want to run higher pressures than suit tubeless systems and the perceived difficulty of using an inner tube in the event of a puncture. Nevertheless, it appears that the systems being pioneered by Hutchinson works well and Shimano is pushing tubeless road wheels so it will come.

CHANGE & UPGRADE
Wheels

Wheels, quite literally, make the cyclist's world go round. Having the right set can make that world travel smoother, faster and safer

The vast majority of bikes are sold fully assembled, aimed at specific price points within the market. Often, the areas where cutbacks are made are the wheels, hence why they're one of the first upgrades cyclists make to their bikes, whether they're road cyclists or mountain bikers. Changing the wheels is the quickest and most effective way of knocking as much as a couple of kilos off your bike's weight, while a good set of wheels can transform its speed and handling, making it accelerate quicker, ascend and descend faster, and even look better.

Road Wheels

Choosing the style of wheel to suit your needs is essential. Most complete bikes are sold with standard, box section rims but a common upgrade is to opt for deeper rims, anything from 35mm to 80mm. The most common depth is around 50mm.

For racing, the tubular wheel is de rigueur for its speed and handling, but requires care and attention when applying the tyre to the rim – either with glue or tape. The most common types of rims are clinchers, where the tyre is held in place with beading. Clinchers are the most popular for everyday riders for their simplicity and are available with either alloy or carbon braking

Deep section rims are more aerodynamic and a useful upgrade for racers or serious sportive riders.

Box section rims are easy to control in cross winds and can save weight.

MTB Wheels

There are a number of different styles of MTB wheels on the market, each to suit a particular style of riding: Downhill, Trail riding or XC Racing. In recent years, mountain biking has seen the emergence of the '29er', a 29" wheel that is well suited to technical situations, offering more confident handling.

Hubs can either be 6-bolt or centre lock, determining the type of disc brake that can be fitted. For general off-road riding, the most common size of rotor is anything

Wheel of fortune?

Wheels can be an expensive purchase, but better quality means better performance and strength.

between 140mm to 180mm, but in the case of more extreme styles of riding, such as downhill or 4X, a 203mm larger rotor is required for.

The 29" wheel, or '29er', is becoming increasingly more popular. The bigger wheels offer greater stability and control off-road.

An all-round mountain bike wheel with center-lock hub is extremely commonplace and suitable for a wide range of tasks.

EDITOR'S TIP

"The 650B wheel looks to break through to the mainstream in the 2013 model year. The 27.5" wheel offers a middle ground between the standard 26" MTB wheel and the en vogue 29er (29" wheel)."

CHANGE & UPGRADE
Tyres

Everything you do when cycling, from pedalling to steering via breaking, comes into effect through the tyres – so choosing the right set is of critical importance

Choosing the correct tyres for a riders' demands is paramount to ensuring a bike handles well, so it's important to look at the wide range available to make the right decision on tyres.

Road Tyres

Your contact with the road surface beneath your wheels is very small on a road bike so it needs little explanation as to why tyres are fundamental to how well a bike performs – the right tyres will make a big difference to speed and the frequency of those dreaded punctures.

Clinchers are the standard type of tyre for road cyclists; it's their usability that is key to their success. Few tools and little know-how allow for easy puncture repairs as the tyre is held in place by beading and once inflated, the beading grips inside the rim of the wheel.

Tubular tyres are rarer than clinchers, and are glued or taped to the rim of a specific tubular wheel. Unlike clinchers they don't have innertubes, thus eliminating friction between tube and tyre, which impedes rolling resistance, making them the choice for racing cyclists.

Time for new tyres? Checking tyres regularly for cuts and wear is highly advised, but upgrades can be made for better puncture protection and less rolling resistance.

EDITOR'S TIP *"For greater road comfort, go for a wider 25c tyre."*

A good quality clincher tyre can be used for all types of riding, from racing through to a daily commute.

Tubular tyres are worth the effort installing for serious racers.

Mountain Bike Tyres

Mountain bikers, year round, are exposed to the elements. They see the changing of the seasons in the leaves, and they also see it flying beneath their tyres – along with significant amounts of grass, gravel, dirt and muddy water. Different depths and degrees of tread on the tyre offer a varying combination of grip, speed and endurance, so matching the right tyre to the correct conditions is essential.

Tubeless tyres are more puncture resistant at low pressures, and are rapidly becoming the tyre of choice among the mountain biking community. Having said that, they usually require greater installation and m tenance work – so maybe not for the beginner.

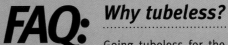

FAQ: **_Why tubeless?_**

Going tubeless for the extra effort installing saves weight, improves handling and increases defence against a race-finishing puncture.

An intermediate tyre for general purpose, good for most conditions and trail riding.

A hardcore tyre for heavy conditions or downhill riding.

A fast tyre, designed specifically for dryer conditions or for cross-country racing.

6

Steering

A good place for the new bicycle mechanic to start

The headset is where virgin mechanics usually start. Headsets loosen on new bikes, making that irritating clunking sound that feels so wrong. You quickly find that an Aheadset is susceptible to logical handling and, as most bearings are sealed these days, it really goes together pretty easily. After a quick tweak with an Allen key, the steering is as smooth as the Venus de Milo's marble bosom and suddenly you're a mechanic! Confidence is all it takes so, when you read that a stem with a little more rise may improve your riding position, you don't think twice about doing the upgrade. And so it goes on until you are changing cups, bearings and forks without a second thought.

"Man made it and man can make it again, you can make it work. Don't panic!"

The secret is to progress a little at a time, to record what you have undone so you can be sure to do it up again and to keep calm. It's only nuts and bolts. Man made it and man can make it again, you can make it work. Have faith.

Headsets and Aheadsets

A clunky looseness or, the opposite, a binding in your steering means the headset bearing needs some care and attention

The good news is that there is almost a standard bearing system for both road and mountain bike steering. That makes all the difference when you come to investing the time and money that is required to master this piece of mechanical skill – you'll use it a lot. The system is not universal (of course). In the old days, bicycle fork steerers (the tube that connects the fork to the stem and handlebars) were always 1 inch in diameter and threaded into the headset, necessitating big spanners. Such a system is now rare, but there are some around, so we'll deal with them later. But the huge majority of modern bikes use a 1 1/8 inch Aheadset. Hurrah! (Although there are, naturally, some downhill mountain bikes beefed up with a 1 1/2 steerer).

The Aheadset

It's a very simple component and easy to service. The system consists of two bearing races positioned at either end of the head tube, held in place by the fork at one end and the stem at the other. Once the bearings have been preloaded by a simple bolt the stem clamps the system together securely. It's very effective and even the cheaper Aheadsets on the market will last a long time if the frame is properly prepared and the unit is serviced regularly.

The assembly

The cylindrical parts of the two cups are pressed into the top and bottom ends of the head tube with the cupped ends carrying the bearings. The crown race sits where the fork meets the steerer tube and turns against the bottom bearing, and the top race does the same against the top bearing. The star-fangled nut is pushed inside the steerer tube where it seats itself allowing the top cap bolt to pull the assembly together and finely adjust the bearing load, while the stem finally clamps them together.

crown race

top cup
(and bearing)

fork washer

top cap

bottom cup
(and bearing)

top race

star-fangled
nut

top cap
bolt

 **KNOW HOW**

Integrated Aheadsets

Integrated or hidden Aheadsets have the bearing pressed directly into the frame, without using cups. Instead the top and bottom of the head tube are flared to accept the bearing parts. Usually fitted at the factory the quality of the frame building dictates how good they are. Not so easy to service and replace as the standard type. The jury is still out.

REPAIR & MAINTENANCE
Aheadset adjustment

Occasionally your headset will work loose; sometimes it will tighten up. It may just need adjustment. Here's how

1 To check the Aheadset, apply the front brake, and rock the bike backwards and forwards. You'll feel or hear a slight knocking if the unit is loose. If you've been running the unit loose for a while, the chances are that the bearings will need replacing – riding with a loose Aheadset will batter the bearings and ruin the surfaces in the unit.

2 It's also possible that the system is too tight or notchy. To check this, pick up the front of the bike and let the bars hang under their own weight. Stiff head-parts won't budge. If the Aheadset is too tight it's unlikely that it'll flop to one side, as shown here. A properly adjusted Aheadset with smooth bearings should have no play and be able to move easily, like this.

3 Loosen the two bolts on the side of the stem. These bolts clamp the stem to the top of the steerer and also keep the Aheadset unit complete.

4 Once you've loosened the bolts, tighten the top cap slightly (this preloads it) to take up any play in the system. You'll only need a small nip to tighten the unit (around 3Nm).

5 Retighten the stem-clamp bolts to the recommended torque setting. Always use a torque wrench especially if you're using a carbon steerer and/or stem.

REPAIR & MAINTENANCE
Servicing Aheadset bearings

Allen keys and grease are all you need. First remove the bars and disconnect the front brake so the forks can be removed and set aside...

 The bearings will either be a sealed cartridge or ball bearings. Both systems are good, but the advantage with loose bearings is that they can be stripped out and re-greased. If the bearings are wearing out regularly, the cups could be out of line in the frame and need to be refitted.

 Once you've serviced the bearings, the forks can be re-installed. Make sure that you return all the seals the right way up, and that you grease the bearings and insert them into the cups the right way around. Don't leave the forks in the bike without returning the stem, even if the friction in the seals appears to be enough to hold them in place.

 There should be a gap between the top of the steerer and the inside top of the Aheadstem of 2–3mm. The gap shouldn't be any bigger than this, as the Aheadstem bolts must be able to tighten over the steerer. If the bolts are above the height of the steerer, the stem will be distorted and won't be tightened to the correct torque figure. The problem isn't just that you might pull the bars off, but the stem will also loosen over time and damage the bearings.

 When you replace the top cap, check that the bottom of the top cap doesn't snag on the top of the steerer. If it does, you may have to place an extra spacer on top of the stem to give a little more space.

EDITOR'S TIP   *"If you unclamp the stem with the top cap bolt out, the fork is quite likely to fall on your foot and it hurts! We've all done it"*

6 Before refitting the handlebars, check that there are no sharp edges around the stem clamp. Also check that you have the right-diameter bars and stem. Most decent handlebar stems, such as the one pictured here, have slightly chamfered edges. Put a dab of copper slip on the stem bolts before replacing them, to prevent them from seizing.

5 Most stems have two clamp bolts, one on either side, so that the stem won't be pulled over to one side as you tighten the bolts. It's critical that you don't over- or under-tighten these bolts. Retighten the sterm clamp bolts to the manufacturer's recommended torque settings – which will be adequate and will mean that the bars will still twist in the event of a crash.

7 Replace the front section of the bar clamp. Number the bolts 1–4 clockwise, then tighten them alternately (e.g. 1–3– 2–4) and to 6–7 Nm. Don't over-tighten the bolts or tighten them too quickly – make sure you reach the desired torque setting gradually. Line the handlebars up and make sure that you've positioned them centrally.

8 Once you've tightened the stem, check that there's an equal gap at the top and bottom between the clamping sections. If there's a difference, tighten or loosen the stem bolts until they match. This is critical, as it'll ensure that there's an equal force on each bolt and that the bar is properly clamped. This is especially important with carbon bars and lightweight aluminium ones.

9 Check that the bars are straight and that the stem is tight. Line the bars up with the front hub. You can hold the wheel between your legs and line the bars up by twisting them. You may need to loosen the stem bolts slightly to make this possible.

Steering

REPAIR & MAINTENANCE
Servicing standard headsets

There are still plenty of these around; indeed, as interest in bikes soars we are seeing renewed interest in classic styles

Standard headsets share similar parts to Aheadsets, especially the frame cups. Installation of the basic frame parts is the same. The main difference is the fitting to the forks and how the stem attaches to the fork.

Headset types for road bikes are fewer than for mountain bikes. Road bikes never had 11⁄8in standard-sized headsets with quill stems – they changed straight over to 1in and 11⁄8in-sized Aheadsets, with 11⁄8in taking over as the 'industry standard' soon after.

The legendary Beryl Burton, serial cycling champion and Britain's most successful female amateur athlete, performed prodigious feats on old school kit

A few manufacturers have stuck with the standard non-integrated-headset look (Seven, Serotta and Colnago) and there's a lot to be said for the standard system (easier to replace and more reliable), although the current trend for smooth integrated head tubes and forks appears to be taking over. Standard quill stems and headsets are now rare, and while there's nothing wrong with them and they work just as well, they require some specialist headset spanners to adjust. The quill stem is less serviceable than an Aheadset, as it's harder to remove the bars without removing the tape and the brake levers. However, the best thing about quill stems is that they offer larger ranges of adjustment than the Aheadset system.

1 The quill stem is held in place with a wedge system that traps the shaft of the stem inside the fork steerer. A 6mm Allen key holds the wedge tight in the end of the stem.

2 Even after the bolt is undone, the stem stays wedged in place – don't undo the bolt completely, but just enough so that the head of the bolt protrudes from the stem.

3 Tap the top of the bolt gently with a plastic mallet, or use a piece of wood to protect the head of the bolt and use a standard hammer.

4 The quill stem system has plenty of adjustment for height, but there's a minimum-insert limit line marked and you mustn't go beyond this. It's worth noting that the height range available with a quill stem is far greater than an Aheadset system.

5 The bolt travels the length of the stem and the wedge is attached to the bottom. It's important not to undo the bolt too far, as the wedge can fall into the stem.

6 The standard 1in headset requires two 32mm headset spanners to undo the locknut. The bottom one traps the forks and prevents them from spinning, then the locknut can be removed.

7 The locknut threads onto the fork steerer, and there's a washer underneath, between the steerer and the top locking nut.

8 The top race sits directly on top of the bearings, which in turn sit inside the top cup. To service the system properly, you'll need to remove the forks and access the bearings at both ends of the headset.

9 The threaded part of steerer has to be cut precisely. This Shimano headset has a sealed bearing unit that can be replaced. Campagnolo headsets (and Aheadsets) still use ball bearings held in cages, which can be cleaned, regreased and replaced.

10 Adjustment is simple but requires the right tools. Once the top race has been threaded onto the forks and nipped up, the locking top nut and washer can be screwed on and into place. Balancing the play and free-running bearing is a question of tightening the race and backing it off against the locking nut.

11 Once you've finished servicing the headset, make sure that you clean and grease the inside of the fork steerer and the wedge-and-quill arrangement before you re-install the stem.

Your local bike shop

The bike trade insists there are only a handful of professional bike shops and the rest are run by amateurs who like bikes. The trade is interested in selling stuff, of course, but it is those shops, run by enthusiasts who care, that we riders enjoy. They're part of what keeps cycling special.

CHANGE & UPGRADE
Fitting Aheadset and forks

This is another of those jobs that become quite easy the third time around. It also requires expensive tools. Time for an objective decision – are you up for it?

To install Aheadsets correctly, you need to prepare your frame carefully and to have some specialist tools. Often, the bike shop will fit the forks and therefore do this preparation work for you, but if you need to do it yourself, it's important to follow the steps below – your bike will ride better and last longer if you do.

Corner cutting
You will meet experienced riders who have never faced off a frame in their lives, who bang off crown races with a hammer and screwdriver and tell you all you need to change a headset is a club hammer and a lump of wood. And yes, it can be done. And, face it, you can do more harm trying to prepare a frame and doing it badly than you can not doing it at all.

They get away with it, if they do, because they're very good mechanics. The less experienced you are the more you need that

Tools:
- pointed bradawl or small screwdriver
- sharp hacksaw
- fork cutting guide
- star-fangled setting tool
- permanent marker
- pen and ruler
- Allen keys
- metal half-round file
- cup-removing tool
- mallet
- crown race removing tool

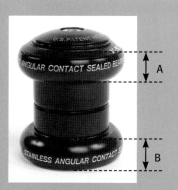

Stack height
I've already mentioned that Aheadsets come in a variety of different sizes (1in, 11/8in and 11/2in), but each manufacturer makes them with a different stack height too. Stack height is the amount of space that the cups take up on the steerer. If you are fitting a new Aheadset, make sure that you buy a similar make or one with the same stack height. If the stack is too high, the stem won't have enough steerer to hold on to. Remember that most forks will be ruined if you cut the steerer too short, as they can't be replaced – so always double-check your measurements before you cut.

solid square press that will push your cups in perfectly straight. My advice: if you're going to do it, do it right and get the tools to back you up.

Fork rake
Road bikes are designed to be used with a specific fork. Fitting the wrong fork can change the steering characteristics quite drastically. Most forks will have their rake marked on them – it's the measurement from the centre line of the head tube to the centre of the fork's dropout – replace like with like unless you want to change the ride.

1 Old headset cups can be removed with a cup-removing tool like this one, which splays out inside the head tube and ensures a snug fit on the inside of the cups. It rests on top of the cups and allows you to tap it out with equal force. Using a long screwdriver is not an option, as it can damage the inside of the frame and ruin the cups.

2 Tap the cup-removing tool with a mallet to remove the cups. With some smaller head tubes it can be tricky to get the tool to fit properly, as the jaws can be restricted by the other race. So, be careful and make sure you wrap a cloth around the cup to prevent it pinging off around the workshop.

3 The crown race is a very delicate component and can also be slightly smaller than the crown of most forks, which can make it difficult to remove. You can remove some crown races by tapping them with a plastic mallet and a suitably soft drift, but it's far better to use a crown race-removing tool, as it won't scratch the forks and damage the crown.

4 The tool pictured here is a dual-purpose cutter. It faces the head tube and also cuts the inside of the tube at the same time, making sure that the Aheadset cups are inserted squarely into the tube. The top and the bottom of the tube are faced – this is to ensure that the cups are parallel so they don't work against each other and wear out quickly. It'll remove any rust or paint on the tube and also make sure the cups are a perfect fit.

5 When you've faced the tube, it'll look perfectly flat and shiny like this one, and the Aheadset cups will fit squarely into the tube. Clean out all the swarf from the inside and grease the top and bottom faces with some anti-seize grease. Grease the inner parts of the cups too, and check they're the right way up (the logos are usually a dead giveaway).

6 Remove any seals from the cups. Insert the cup so that it's straight and can't distort as you push it in with the headset press tool – the cups usually have a shamfered edge to guide them into the tube.

7 It's best to do one cup at a time to avoid damage and so you can line up the logos. Some cups have grease-guard ports, which should face to the side so you can get to them easily. The tool simply (and quickly) forces the cups into the head tube – don't try to install a headset with a hammer, as this won't work.

8 Now the top cup can go in. The tool has a variety of dies that fit different-sized cups. Make sure that you use one that fits well but not too snugly, as the force on the tool can make it seize onto the aluminium cup and ruin it. You'll find that the cups will be easier to install if the head tube has been cut and faced. Finally, inspect the cups closely to check that they're flush with the tube (hold the bike up to the light and see if there are any gaps).

Cutting forks

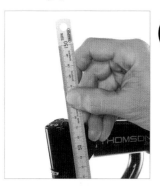

1 It's best to measure the old fork steerer with a ruler first and then compare it with the old forks once you've marked them, otherwise you'll have to assemble the whole system before cutting the new fork. This is essential if you are changing position or fitting a different type of Aheadset or stem.

2 Mark the steerer with a permanent marker pen, as you'll have to insert the forks into the head tube before it's cut. Alternatively, use a vernier calliper and measure the amount you need to remove, then add 2mm to account for the recess required to fit the top cap.

3 Next, fit the fork crown race. Most forks will have factory-cut crowns, but some need facing for a perfect fit – there's a workshop tool to do this job if necessary, which knocks the crown race onto the crown – make sure that the adaptor is a good fit to the race and remove any rubber or plastic seals before you do this, as they can be damaged.

Bike clubs

You don't have to buy all the more expensive tools yourself – that is what bike clubs are for. Very often the club will have its own workshop. If not, get together with a group of riders and try to persuade the club to buy the tools to loan or hire to members. Or a group of you can buy them between you. We're talking a few hundred pounds, not thousands. British Cycling have a list of clubs on their website: *http://new.britishcycling.org.uk*

"Enjoy working on your bike. It's very satisfying to get it right and it's not something you can do with your car or most of the machines you own these days"

4 At this point, assemble the complete system, including bearings, to check you have the steerer at the right length. Although you may not want to cut the steerer twice, it may be better if you're not sure how high you want the bars.

5 It's better to allow for more spacers if you are unsure how high you want your bars. If I'm assembling a bike for someone else, I always leave 30mm of spacers under the stem so that the rider can decide. The steerer can always be cut again after a test ride.

6 Cut the steerer to length using a sharp new hacksaw blade, holding the steerer in a cutting guide to stop the blade wandering as you cut. It's essential that the cut is square to ensure that the stem fits properly and the 'star nut' (see step 8) can be installed easily. If you are cutting a carbon-fibre steerer, wear a facemask.

7 File off any burrs on the outside and inside of the steerer tube. Take care not to scratch the steerer and make sure that the edges of the tube won't scratch the inside of the stem when you replace it. The inside has to be clear so that the top cap nut can be easily inserted inside the tube.

8 On steel and aluminium steerers, the star nut is the fixed part of the system which allows the stem top cap to fasten down on the headset stack, so that you can adjust out any play in the bearing.
NB: They're not recommended for carbon-fibre steerers and may be difficult to fit to some aluminium steerers with thicker tube walls.

9 Use a star nut setting tool, as pictured here, and you can't fail to get it set straight in the steerer.

10 Once inserted, star nuts are very hard to remove, as they fit by wedging themselves into the inside of the tube. This scratches the tube, so removing the nut can make a big mess of both the nut and the steerer. If the star-fangled nut is damaged or seized, simply knock it further down the steerer and fit a replaceable wedge.

11 Alternatively, you can use a replaceable top cap and wedge. I prefer to use one of these removable top-cap wedges – these units are inserted and tightened into the steerer with an Allen key.

12 Once tightened into the steerer, these units are safer and can be refitted, which is really important if you don't have a star nut setting tool. They also can't damage the inside of the steerer tube, so can be used on carbon steerers. But, best of all, they're also less likely to rust and seize, as you can remove them and clean them up.

13 Expandable wedges like this are essential in carbon steerers as star nuts can damage carbon steerers irreparably.

14 The stem must fit with a recess of 2–3mm of steerer – this allows for adjustment and for the top cap to fit. Then adjust the stem and tighten all the bolts to the manufacturer's recommended torque settings.

CHANGE & UPGRADE
Handlebars & Stems

The quality of your steering setup has a huge impact on your comfort, safety and enjoyment on both road and trail. Ensuring you have the right components is the first step to success

Before trying to buy speed with expensive lightweight carbon frames and wheels, it's worth spending time with a tape measure to get a position on your bike that suits you and, should you be lucky enough to own more than one cycle, then replicate it across your range of bikes. Sitting too upright is detrimental to speed, but so is pain and discomfort (from an overly aggressive position).

Road Handlebars & Stems

Various styles of road handlebars fill the shops, but the greatest trend amongst the bike brands in recent times is the compact handlebar (below). It's shorter in reach, meaning the rider isn't stretching too far to hold the brake hoods, and the drop – the lowest part of the handlebar – is shallower, allowing for riding in a more aerodynamic position.

Keeping the stem as long as possible will aid greater control and handling of the bike, but stem length is extremely important; a little adjustment can have a significant impact on your riding position.

FAQ: *Why go Compact?*

Easier to reach drops make it more comfortable to ride in an energy saving aerodynamic position for longer.

Fit the correct length stem, size makes a lot of difference to comfort and control.

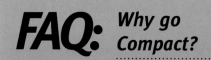

Compact handlebars are user friendly and ideal for less flexible riders.

Mountain Bike Handlebars & Stems

There are different varieties of mountain bike handlebars, each offering characteristics for different disciplines, and while a riser bar is more suited to trail and downhill riding, XC riders often adopt flat bars.

Wide handlebars give greater control off-road, but it's worth taking into consideration the types of conditions and areas the bike is most likely to be ridden in. Having wide bars increases the likelihood of catching a passing tree on narrow trails (for example), so anything over 700mm may prove a little extreme.

Short stems are ideal for steep downhill sections, the position encourages riders to get their weight back

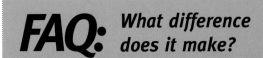

FAQ: **What difference does it make?**

Picking the right bars to suit will improve handling, enabling riders to tackle technical terrain with greater confidence.

on the bike, helping steering, whereas lengths of around 80/90mm are preferred for trail and cross country riding.

This style of bar and stem combination is very popular, the paring of 700mm handlebars and 80mm stem is perfect for trail riding.

UPGRADE...
Rotors

When rotors heat up, their performance deteriorates. Increase stopping power by investing in better quality materials.

Fiber Grip:
Fiber grip is a paste designed to create friction between clamped carbon fibre surfaces. Apply to handlebars, stems and seat posts before installation.

Torque Wrench:
A torque wrench is a specifically designed instrument for applying the correct amount of torque to a bolt, usually specified by the manufacturer.

Teflon Grease: Teflon grease should be applied to adjoining metal components, such as handlebars and stems, before installing them on the bike. The paste prevents the metals forging together over time and can be used on any adjoining metals, even bottle cage bolts.

Brakes

The better your brakes the faster you go

The need for powerful and reliable stopping power when riding down a mountain in mud and slop is paramount and, as you would expect, mountain bike brakes have pushed ahead of standard road callipers to become very specialised and effective. Even the powerful V-brake which set a new MTB standard not so long ago has largely been supplanted by hydraulic disc brakes and the increase in control and ease of use is enormous. The road bike too has seen improvements in the past decade with dual pivot designs maximising pressure at the wheel. No doubt hydraulic discs

"Hydraulic disc brakes have brought an enormous advance in control and ease of use"

will find their way onto road bikes in time, but only when extra efficiency justifies the weight on what is, after all the speed machine of cycling.

Mountain bike disc brakes

A lot of research has gone into developing powerful brakes for mountain bikes, much of it yet to be developed for road...

Tools:
- pointed bradawl or small screwdriver
- torx (star-shaped) key
- torque wrench
- Loctite
- long (needle-nose) pliers

Cable-activated disc brakes

Many entry- and mid-range mountain bikes come with cable discs and, if you set them up properly and maintain them well, they can be just as effective as hydraulic brakes. They also mean you can start off with efficient brakes for less initial outlay. Like hydraulics, cable discs are far easier to look after than V-brakes or cantilevers, and they work much better in the mud. Cable discs can also be serviced without having to buy hydraulic oils and getting messy, so in some situations (such as world tours or adventure rides) it's a lot more convenient to carry spares and re-adjust the brakes with a cable set-up.

Disc brakes sound (and look) complicated, but high-quality disc brake systems are the easiest things to set up and service. There is a variety of different standards for fitting to your bike and there is also a range of hub systems. Hydraulic disc brakes are now lightweight and incredibly efficient, and are sealed to the elements so will always give you predictable, sharp braking. The cables don't need constant attention after wet rides and the callipers also require little readjustment once they have been set up.

Look no brakes

The latest fashion for fixed gear bikes has put brakes into a new perspective. With a fixed wheel, although you must have them by law, you don't strictly need a brake, controlling your speed through the pedals. The first thing you learn is that if you look far enough ahead you hardly need to brake at all, which is something you can take to your general riding. The second thing is that brakes actually give you speed – you just can't fly down a hill at full thrash without them. So brakes make you go faster, who'd have thought it?

REPLACE & UPGRADE
Cable disc set-up

The advantages of a disc brake at a more reasonable price

1 Fit the disc rotors to the hubs. These Shimano rotors have washers that are designed to secure the bolt and prevent it from undoing completely. Many HGV lorries have a similar device to keep their wheel bolts in check. Also check that the rotor direction arrows are pointing in the direction of rotation. You should check that these bolts are tight on a regular basis. Use some Loctite on the bolts if you remove or replace the discs, as undoing the bolt will damage the thread lock.

2 Tighten the rotor bolts to 4 Nm. Turn the bolts a quarter-turn only at a time, working gradually on opposite or alternate bolts until you reach the desired torque setting. Do not tighten up one bolt completely and then the next, as doing these bolts up unevenly and in one go can distort the rotor.

3 Once the rotor is in place you can 'set' the washers by bending them to sit flat with the head of the rotor bolt, which is three-sided. This is an added precaution that prevents the bolts from vibrating loose. Once the disc is installed, leave it for a few hours before you ride to give the Loctite a chance to set properly.

4 Secure the brake calliper to the fork or frame. Add some Loctite to the bolts and tighten them to make them secure. It is important to realise that tightening each bolt equally and to the right torque setting is far more important than just doing them up as tight as you can. The Loctite is for additional safety and to prevent the bolts from vibrating loose.

EDITOR'S TIP *"The one thing that detracts from the performance of a brake like this is friction in the cable. Keep them clean and lubricated for powerful braking on a budget."*

 The calliper on Shimano and Avid brakes is very easy to adjust – you simply centre the disc pads over the rotor. The calliper is mounted on slotted bolt-holes, which allow a fair bit of side-to-side movement; this means that this type of calliper can be fitted to forks or frames that do not have perfectly aligned brake bosses. However, it is still a good idea to have the brake bosses faced.

 Pull the cable through the calliper with either a pair of pliers or a cable puller. This will make sure that the cable is in the correct position and that the slack is out of the lever.

 Tighten the Allen key bolt on the brake calliper to 7 Nm. Although this bolt needs to be tight enough to prevent the cable from slipping through the clamp, if it is too tight it can crush and damage the cable, causing it to fray around the clamp. Once the cable is attached, you can stretch the cables and double-check the cable tension.

 To 'bed' the cables in and stretch the system, pull hard on the brake lever several times. This will also check you have done the bolts up tightly enough. Repeat steps 6 and 7 if the cable has slipped at all, or if there is excessive movement in the lever. You can then set the cable tension perfectly by using the adjusting screw on either the brake lever or the calliper, as shown here.

9 The throw of the disc calliper can be fine-tuned using the adjustment screw on the back of the calliper unit. Avid has a red button to twist for this adjustment. Be careful to check that the throw is tuned as the pads wear; this will ensure progressive pad wear and braking effectiveness. Check all the bolts on the calliper regularly as they can vibrate loose over time.

10 Finally, check all the torque settings on the rotor bolts and callipers and test the brakes before you ride. Bed the pads in so that they don't glaze up. Make sure that the cables are all tidy – you can use electrical ties to keep the cables out of the way. Check that the cables can't get caught in the suspension forks as you steer, and bounce the forks up and down a few times to check they can't snag on the cables.

Centering the brakes

To centre the brakes quickly with the cable already installed, undo both of the angle-adjusting bolts. Pull the brake into the full-on position and tie a toe strap or zip tie around the brake to hold it in place. Tighten the angle bolts with the brake applied. Undo the tie and spin the wheel, which should be spot-on. Then tweak the pad alignment.

REPLACE & UPGRADE
Disc brake pads
Pads wear out, can be contaminated by careless use of lubricants and will need replacing regularly...

Fitting new disc callipers does take time to get right. However, if you use the recommended rotors, hubs and levers, they will work far better. Once they have been set up correctly, replacing disc pads is really easy.

The callipers for the front and rear brakes are different sizes, so make sure you have the correct calliper before you start. There are two types of disc calliper fixing systems too – ISO two-bolt and pillar-mounted (the latter are used on Manitou forks and some Shimano brakes). Rotors also come in a variety of sizes depending on the system you are using.

Tools:
- pointed bradawl or small screwdriver
- torque wrench
- brake-mount facing tool (Hope or Magura)
- Allen keys
- disc-brake cleaner
- needle-nose pliers
- grease

1 Most disc brake problems are due to uneven mounting. Have your frame checked out using Magura's 'Gnann-o-mat'; this tool will remove any extra material from wonky bosses, placing the calliper in line with the rotor and the hub.

2 The callipers must be centred over the rotor, rather than over the pads themselves, to make sure that the pads wear evenly and to prevent vibration and any nasty noises. Make sure that the wheel is tight in the frame.

3 To fine-tune the spacing between the pad and the rotor, you can add shims to the mount on either the fork or the frame. These are available in a variety of sizes (0.2 mm, 1 mm, 2 mm and 3 mm).

4 Once you're happy that the rotor is centred in the calliper and the faces are square, tighten the fixing bolts. Refer to the manufacturer's recommended torque settings. You may need a few tries to get it drag-free but it's worth it.

5 Shimano XTR and XT discs have a threaded pin with a split pin on one end to retain the bolt should it start to shake loose. If this pin pops out, you can expect brake failure and a potentially nasty accident, so put them back correctly!

6 Hayes pads use a retaining spring rather than a magnet to secure the pad to the top of the cylinder. This is very easy to locate and snaps in and out instantly. Make sure the pads are properly replaced before returning the wheel.

Types of pad

Organic pads

Once fitted, organic compound pads need 'breaking in' before you ride them properly off-road. To do this, find a hill and do twenty firm 'stops' from about 20–30 km/h. This stabilises the compound and prevents the pads from disintegrating under pressure or wearing quickly.

Sintered pads

Sintered pads don't need to be broken in. They are very slightly heavier and get hotter than organic compound pads and therefore shouldn't be used in some brake systems (such as Magura), so always read the instructions! Sintered pads work very well, but they do wear the rotor out more quickly than organic-type pads.

Mixing pads and pad wear

Some riders experiment with mixing different types of pads in the callipers to alter brake feel and performance. Check regularly for wear. Once the pad is worn out, you risk brake failure and a nasty accident should the base of the pad catch on the rotor.

 7 Pads that use a split pin rather than a retaining spring need careful attention. Once you have straightened out the splayed ends using a pair of needle-nose pliers, you can pull the pin out.

 8 When you have removed the split pin, squeeze the pads together and pull them out of the calliper. You can then clean the calliper with disc brake cleaner and inspect the cylinders inside the calliper for any leaks or wear.

 9 These Shimano pads have a leaf spring in between the two pads. The spring is easy to replace as it has a hole in the top of it that matches up with either side of the calliper and the pads. Return the new pads and replace the split pin.

 10 Whatever system you have, it's always worth checking that the calliper hasn't moved since you last replaced the pads. This type of post-mounted rear calliper is very simple to centre as it is mounted on slotted bolt-holes.

 11 Finally, thoroughly clean the brake rotor with rotor cleaner. Do not use a water-repelling spray lube or anything with oil in it. The pads contaminate very easily and the smallest amount of grease (even hamburger fat!) can ruin a new set of pads.

EDITOR'S TIP *"When you use a spray can on or around your bike, be very aware of where the spray can reach. An ill directed blast of lube onto your brake pads means a lot of time wasted trying to clean them and probably the cost of a new set when you fail. Best to cover them before you start."*

FAQ: *Is there some curse that stops me getting my disc brakes to work perfectly?*

If it feels like that it may be that the brake mounts are out of line. Have them checked and if it's not get everything ground parallel.

Rotor wear

Rotors do wear out eventually. However, they last a lot longer if you refresh your pads regularly and keep the callipers and rotors clean. Just like rims, rotors can buckle, usually due to excessive heat build up or lack of care when throwing them into the back of the car. If this happens, your brakes will drag and slow you down. Remember that the rotor-to-pad spacing is around 0.5 mm so it won't take much of a buckle to mess it all up, not to mention wear pads out faster and provide irregular performance. Change the rotors if they are damaged to keep your brakes safe.

Rotor performance

Wavy rotors are becoming more popular. They keep the pads slightly cooler than standard

round rotors and prevent the heat that builds up in the pistons from cooking the brake fluid. This build up can have a dramatic effect on brake performance and make the brakes fade under pressure on long downhills. Wavy discs also 'shave' the pads and thus prevent the glaze on the pad from building up. The result is faster pad wear but more efficient braking performance.

Quick-release levers

On all disc brake systems, make sure that you use a good-quality quick-release lever, preferably made of steel – Shimano quick releases are particularly good. Then tighten the lever firmly and check it regularly.

CHANGE & UPGRADE
Hydraulic disc brakes

Fear of bleeding hydraulic systems keeps too many riders from enjoying top brake performance

Hydraulic disc brakes terrify most home mechanics, but the truth is they are possibly the easiest thing to set up and service. They have the advantage over rim brakes in that once they are set up properly, they need little effort to retain consistent and predictable braking, and they are far better than a cable system as the 'cables' on hydraulic brakes perform better and don't require any attention.

Setting up hydraulic disc brakes, bleeding the system and changing hoses can be messy, so make sure you do this in a suitable environment and put something on the floor to soak up spillage. Wear an apron and some silicone rubber gloves, as brake fluid is not kind to your skin.

Why bleed a disc brake?

The mushy, weak feeling at the brakes is due to air caught in the system. The disc systems on many new bikes need bleeding because there will be a lot of air in the hoses. This air will not just affect the feel at the lever, but will also absorb power. Therefore, your brakes will lose power and modulation, so bleeding is

Tools:
- brake fluid (follow your bike manufacturer's recommendations)
- 8 mm ring spanner
- syringe and fluid piping
- bleed kits (the ones with syringes are the simplest to use as they allow you to regulate the flow of liquid and keep an eye on how much fluid you have left to flush through. However, bleed kits aren't totally essential, and as you get more confident you will no doubt develop your own techniques.

essential for peak performance.

The Shimano system uses mineral oil, not DOT4 or 5.1 fluid. Do not mix fluids and always use the manufacturer's recommended fluid. Don't mix bleed kits either, as DOT fluid can be corrosive and can contaminate mineral oil kits, while mineral oils do not damage your paintwork. DOT fluid is very bad for your skin. Performance wise, there's not a lot in it.

Using a bleed kit

 1 Turn the brake lever so that the reservoir on the handle is level with the ground. Then remove the cover and the rubber plate (or diaphragm) underneath. This will expose the fluid and the piston chamber next to the lever. Wind out the lever-reach adjusters so that the pistons will allow enough fluid into the system.

 2 Centre the hole in the bleed clamp cover over the reservoir, which has a foam seal on it that clamps up to leave your hands free and prevent any fluid escaping. Hook the overflow bottle on the handlebars and you're ready to bleed. This is a Shimano bleed kit, but it can be used on other systems.

3 You need to leave the pads in place while you bleed the system so you can feel the action during the process and once you've finished. Cover the pads with a clean cloth and make sure that no fluid can contaminate the rotor or the disc pads. Contaminated pads must be replaced. Some systems come with a spacer to use instead of the rotor and pads – use this if you have one as it will ensure the pads do not get contaminated.

Want more power?
Fit bigger rotors

Use some brake adapters to space your callipers away from the centre of the hub. This means that you can fit bigger rotors while still using your existing callipers. You can therefore increase braking power by up to 35 per cent.

4 Place the hose of the full syringe over the bleed nipple on the calliper, then open the valve with a spanner. Slowly push the oil into the system, then pull the brake lever carefully two or three times to bed everything in. Continue pushing until there's about 10 cc left in the syringe, then jiggle the plunger back and forth so it's free of air. Finally, pull the plunger back slightly to suck some fluid back.

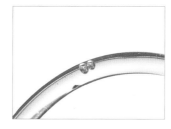

5 The excess oil will pass through the tube on the bleed clamp and into the bottle. Stop when the fluid runs clear, without any bubbles in it.

6 Now check the 'bite' of the brake – that is, where the pads hit the rotor. It should feel positive and smooth without any give at the levers. If it still feels mushy, pump the lever several times and repeat step 4 to make sure the air is out of the system. Top up the reservoir so it is full to the top edge of the unit. Be careful not to introduce any air bubbles, which may mean you have to start again.

7 Replace the rubber cover and the reservoir cap and tighten the screws. Clean any excess fluid off the handlebars, levers and grips with some disc cleaning fluid. Dispose of any used fluid properly – ask your local bike shop where they take theirs, or call the local waste authority. Do not pour brake fluid, or any non-water-soluble oils, down the drain.

FAQ: *How do I remove paint from my car?*

Just spill some brake fluid over it while you're bleeding your brakes!

Brakes

Or try the quick-bleed method...

 1 Follow steps on 1 and 2 (previous page), then make an overflow bucket using an old drinks bottle and a coat hanger. You can also just wrap a plastic bag over the handlebars (many pro-team mechanics do this), but this creates a lot of mess and there's no way of storing the waste fluid easily.

2 Fill a syringe with bubble-free fluid. Place a tube onto the calliper bleed nipple. Undo the valve nut and then simply push the fluid slowly and steadily through the syringe, to purge the system from the bottom to the top. One full syringe will refresh the system. Then tighten the nipple, follow steps 6 and 7 (previous page) and you're done.

FAQ: *Will moving up to hydraulic disc brakes improve the ride of my bike?*

Infinitely. Reliable controllable stopping power makes everything easier.

Pad care

When cleaning your bike or removing the wheels for transport, always remove the brake pads and set them away from any brake fluid, lube or grease. Then insert a spacer into the calliper to prevent the pistons from popping out should the lever be activated by accident. Leave the pads brake-faces together to make it even more difficult to contaminate the surfaces.

Mushy brakes – a quick-fix tip

If you don't have a bleed kit or you are short of fluid, try this quick fix. Flatten the reservoir and open the cap. Fix the brake in the full-on position with a zip tie and leave for 20–30 minutes. All the bubbles will slowly rise from inside the system. When this has finished, top up the reservoir with extra bubble-free fluid and replace the cover. The result will be sharp lever action and no mushy feel, without having to re-bleed.

 *"Personally I go for a system like Shimano's which uses mineral oil. DOT fluid is corrosive and bad for the skin."*

CHANGE & UPGRADE
Removing & replacing hydraulic brake hoses

Replacing worn hoses with top-of-the-range brands and tailoring them to your bike requires a little bit of sophisticated plumbing...

All hydraulic hoses follow the same replacement principles. Like bleeding, it's pretty simple to do. However, there are a few different types depending on which system you are using. Goodridge hoses are the best available for all systems. They use braided hoses, which are more expensive than normal hoses but give you better braking performance and a less spongy feel at the lever.

Choosing the right length
They are also easier to trim and fit. Some brake line systems have factory-fitted collars, which cannot be cut. You will therefore have to specify the length of hose you need for your bike. With these systems, unlike cable-activated brakes, the amount of hose is less important to the feel at the lever. However, really long plastic runs do tend to flex slightly under heavy braking. Each hose kit (enough for one brake) consists of two banjos, fixing bolts, collars, a length of hose and some O-rings. Check the manufacturer's instructions for recommended tightening torques

and correct hose types before you start. Also, read through the section on bleeding as you will need to do this after the hoses have been installed. Remove any brake pads and make sure that the pistons inside the callipers are flush with the inside of the calliper body. Insert a spacer into the cavity to prevent the pistons from moving.

Dealing with brake fluid
Be careful when you remove the old hose not to splash brake fluid and, although there won't be much fluid in the system, make sure you catch any waste. Wear some gloves and safety goggles as the

Tools:
- 8 mm spanner
- sharp knife
- sharp cable cutters (shearing type)
- hacksaw (sharp)
- bradawl
- bleeding kit
- a sponge and some kitchen roll
- goggles and gloves

fluid is not too kind to your skin. Lastly, always check the hose for leaks before you ride. Tighten all the fittings and squeeze the levers hard. Leave the bike overnight and check for leaks the following day.

What is brake fluid?
Mountain bike brakes generally use DOT 4, DOT 5.1 (glycol-ether based) or Mineral Oil. We don't advise mixing any of them although DOT 4 and 5.1 don't contaminate one another. Mineral Oil doesn't mix with any of the others. Neither does DOT 5, the dangerous one, which is mentioned here so you can avoid having it foisted on you by some ignoramus in place of 5.1. It's silicon based and will ruin your system. Brake fluids are formulated to have high boiling point, constant viscosity and low compressibility. The glycol-ether based versions need careful handling, taking the paint off everything and damaging your skin.

Magura brakes

With Magura brakes you need to push a barbed tubing insert into the open end of the cable. This can be tapped in with a plastic mallet. Use Magura brake blood for Magura hydraulic systems.

 1 Cut braided hoses with a set of sharp cable shears. You can also use a hacksaw with a sharp blade. Measure the new hose against the old one, or cut the hose after you have installed one end securely. Always double-check the length before you cut.

 2 Cut back the plastic covering 11 mm down the hose. This will allow the outer collar to fit snugly over the braided part.

 3 With a clean bradawl or 'podger', make sure that the internal PTFE (Teflon) liner is open enough to allow you to start inserting the spigot part at the end of the banjo.

 4 The exposed braid will now fit into the collar. Be careful as you start to feed the hose into the collar not to fray the braid or trap it over the edge of the collar.

5 Push the collar down the hose, leaving a gap so the collar can rotate freely and thread easily onto the banjo spigot. The spigot has a tapered end to make insertion to the PTFE liner easier.

 6 As the banjo reaches the threaded part of the collar, start to turn the collar to thread it onto the banjo. As the banjo travels further down the hose you will need more force to turn it. If you have to use pliers, cover them with duct tape or electrical tape to prevent them damaging the banjo.

 **EDITOR'S TIP** *"To my mind braided hoses, such as those made by Goodridge, give the best braking performance."*

7 Continue to thread the banjo into the hose, retightening the collar as necessary until it has butted up to the end of the plastic cover. When the banjo has butted up to the end of the collar, lock off the collar against it.

8 Two O-rings per banjo seal the system. The fixing bolt has a hole drilled down the centre and through the middle, which allows fluid to pass into the hose from either the calliper or the lever reservoir. The hose needs to be attached carefully.

9 On XTR levers there are two prongs that locate on either side of the banjo collar. You may have to adjust the collar slightly so that the banjo can sit flat and square through these prongs and onto the lever.

10 Set the angle of the hose before you fix the other end at the lever. Make sure that there is as smooth a line as possible, to ensure that the hose doesn't kink at the collar.

11 When fitting the banjo assembly with a straight-fitting lever, fit the non-banjo type fitting first. This makes it easier to align the banjo at the calliper to the correct angle with the final turn of the spanner.

12 Lastly, once the angles have been set on the banjos and the hoses are the right length, tighten up the collars and the banjo fixing bolts. You can then bleed the system to recharge it with brake fluid.

KNOW HOW

Hope brake lines

Hope systems use a brass olive fitting over the hose outer and a spigot that is pushed into place. This olive is locked onto the lever with a sleeve. All the same rules apply, but be careful when replacing the spigot as it is very fragile and can easily snap off. Hope systems also use DOT 5.1 hydraulic brake fluid.

Mountain bike rim brakes

For many years the most powerful brake around, the V-brake, is still doing a good job on older and budget mountain bikes...

The V-brake is the most powerful cable-activated rim-brake design. It can provide a variety of set-up problems, and care is needed when adjusting them. Servicing your V-brakes on a regular basis is essential – they have to be looked after carefully if you want to get the best performance from them. Regularly removing the brakes from the bike and thoroughly cleaning all the parts (using an old toothbrush to clean the mechanism) will keep them smooth. Lubricate all the

pivots with a dry lube, taking care not to contaminate the pads, and make sure there is no rust on the steel parts. V-brakes are particularly sensitive to water and can seize up if neglected for long periods. So, as with most components on a mountain bike, they need to be prepared properly.

It's important to use the correct, V-brake-compatible brake lever. Using the wrong lever (with too much leverage) can be very dangerous; the V-brake lever is designed to provide the right

Tools:
- pointed bradawl or small screwdriver
- emery cloth
- grease
- 5 mm Allen key
- needle nose pliers
- torque wrench

amount of leverage with two-finger braking. The position of the gear cable nipple in relation to the pivot point and the amount of cable that it pulls in one go are critical.

First things first: releasing your V-brakes
Unhooking the V-brakes will allow you to remove the wheels. The brake callipers will fall apart to allow the fat tyre to clear the pads.

1 Squeeze the two brake arms firmly together so that the pads touch the rims. This should be enough to slacken the cable and allow the noodle to fall out.

2 With your free hand grab the noodle and pull it sideways and away from the opposite calliper. This will pop the head of the noodle out of the retaining cage. Pull the cable through the cage slot.

3 When replacing the noodle, it is essential to make sure that the noodle head is placed securely into the retaining cage. It is possible for the noodle to snag on the edge of the cage giving the impression that it's seated. That is hazardous so double check.

4 This is what the V-brake should look like when reassembled.

Looking after the MTB V-brake

1 Prepare the cantilever studs on the frame. If they are rusty, or if the brakes are a little rough and notchy in their action, you may need to clean off the stud with emery cloth. Use fine grade for a smooth finish.

2 Grease the faces of the canti-stud, as it acts as a pivot for the brake; some brakes have their own bearings or bushes on the stud which benefit from cleaning and greasing too.

3 The frame, or fork, canti-stud will have up to three small holes in it on the inside of the stud. These holes retain the stopper pin on the back of the brake, securing the brake and enabling the spring to act against the brake lever to return the brake to the open position. On cantilever brakes, this can be used to put more return spring into the action. All V-brakes should be used with the one centrally positioned hole.

4 The fixing bolts have a locking compound that prevents them vibrating loose under braking forces. I would suggest squirting a little thin oil into the canti-stud, especially if you have had to re-tap the threads. This will prevent the threads from rusting up. Copper slip is also good for this as it is very hard to wash away.

5 Finally, tighten the fixing bolts to around 7 Nm using a torque wrench. This will need to be re-checked once in a while as vibrations can shake the bolts loose.

6 Make sure that the pads are set just below the top of the rim (about 2 mm), and are flat to act upon all the braking surface of the rim. Check that the pads are facing in the right direction and are on the right calliper arm.

KNOW HOW

Clean rims

Clean rims will make a huge difference to brake performance. Use disc-brake cleaner to clean your rims and regularly remove all the grime that builds up, as brake dust will just act as an abrasive and wear down both the rim and the pads.

REPAIR & MAINTENANCE
Adjusting V-brake blocks

When set up properly, centered and parallel to the braking surface of the rim with the right amount of toe in, V-brakes provide awesome stopping power

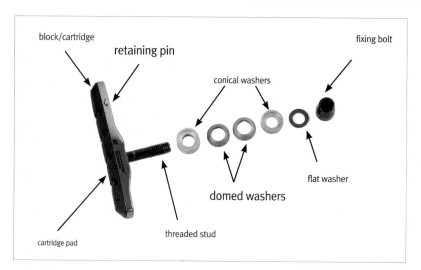

block/cartridge

retaining pin

conical washers

fixing bolt

domed washers

flat washer

threaded stud

cartridge pad

1 The pad is fully adjustable for angles as the retaining washers and spacers act as a ball joint. Make sure that the wheel is centred in the bike before you start.

2 Loosely fit the pads to the rim. The distance between the noodle-retaining cage and the fastening bolt should be over 39 mm.

3 To adjust the pad angle, hold the pad in place with one hand and the Allen key in the other. Make small adjustments and always keep the pads symmetrical. If the pads are hard to adjust or will not stay in place, check that the domed washers are installed correctly. Tighten to 9-10 Nm.

4 There is some 'toe-in' set on these pads, which allows the pad to be 'sucked in' towards the rim as the brake is applied. Set the cables so that there is a gap of about 1–2 mm on either side of the rim, then adjust the spring tension screw to pull the brake central.

5 Once the pads are tight and set at the correct angle and height, you can centre the brake. This will affect how the brake feels at the lever, so check that is still feels easy to apply the brakes. Give the brake a few hard pulls to check that it returns and that the wheel can spin without rubbing.

REPAIR & MAINTENANCE
Replacing cartridge-type pads

This type of pad allows you to replace the rubber part only, the aluminium backing stays put so it only needs setting up once and allows you to change the pads quickly

1 Once the brake shoe is in place, pad replacement is simple as the only part that has to be moved is the pad. Pull out the split pin from the top of the shoe. Replace the pin too.

2 Slide the pad out of the shoe – pads tend to be quite loose fitting so this should be easy. Replace the pad and make sure you are using the correct pad.

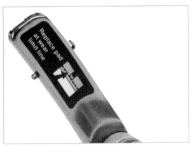

3 The pin must be inserted so that it is visible on either side of the shoe. You will know that it is properly installed as it will be easy to push all the way through. If it won't go in easily, slide the pad back and forth a little until the pin 'pops' into place. The spring in the pin retains the pad, making sure it doesn't drop out.

KNOW HOW

Wet and dry

V-brake pads wear fairly evenly and slowly in dry conditions. However, in the wet you can wear through a set in a matter of hours, especially if it's muddy. As V-brake pads are usually very low profile, they wear out in a matter of months in the summer and weeks in the winter. If you want razor-sharp braking from V-brakes, fit some ceramic rims and ceramic-compatible pads.

Squealing

Squealing is caused by vibration. As the pad hits the rim it applies friction to slow the wheel down. The result of this friction is vibration and a build-up of heat. This wears down the brake pads and can also create a hell of a racket. Toe in the pads and you'll alleviate the problem. However, if this still doesn't work there may be excessive play in the brake assembly and it may need to be replaced.

Ceramic rims

Ceramic rims are a great idea for V-brakes if you are having trouble stopping. They do require special pads, as standard rubber pads can wreck the surface, glazing it up and making it unusable.

REPAIR & MAINTENANCE
V-brake cables

Cables are the most vulnerable element of a braking system; they need care if they're to transfer maximum power from lever to brake...

You should check for cable trouble on a regular basis and always take care of your cables when releasing the brakes to remove the wheels, as they are vulnerable and susceptible to kinking. Kinked cables and water inside the outers will slow your braking down considerably. It's hard to tell when the inner wire is kinked, but a sloppy or stiff feeling in the lever action is a dead give-away. Replacing the cable run is the best way to solve this, but stripping out the inner and using a quality spray

lube can be a short-term fix. It's pretty rare for a brake cable to fray dangerously, but it's worth checking the inner cable, especially if the brakes are feeling stiffer than usual. This friction can be caused by the inner cable rubbing on either a burr on the outer cable or a frame cable stop. It's also rare for cables to snap, but they can fray at the clamp bolts which can make future adjustment difficult.

You can adjust cable tension at the levers 'on the fly' using the adjusters on the lever at the

handlebar. Simply unscrew the centre section and the inner cable will tighten. Then lock it off with the outer lock ring. Check the lever a few times and make sure you have left enough play for the wheel to spin freely. We ran through lever reach in section 2. However, adjusting the reach can affect the pull of the brake lever, so long-term adjustment of the slack in a cable system is best done by pulling the cable through at the brake-cable fastening bolt on the calliper.

1 Cables can be removed quickly by turning the adjustment screw on the lever so that the slot faces forward and lines up with the slot in the brake lever body. Release the brakes at the callipers and then pull gently on the lever. As you release the lever, the cable will slacken and the inner cable can be fed through this slot.

2 The nipple can then be unhooked from the lever. Be careful when you return the cables and make sure that the cables are properly relocated into the adjusters, noodles and frame stops, so that they cannot slip out when the brake is applied.

 **3** Mountain bike brake cables have a barrel nipple that rotates slightly in the lever every time you pull on the brakes. Greasing the nipple will prevent friction and stop any noises developing as the levers are applied. Inspect the nipples regularly and check for any signs of wear and tear on the cable around the nipple.

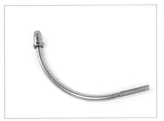 **4** The cable noodle pipe comes in two lengths. The shorter (90-degree) one is for the rear brakes and the longer (170-degree) one is for the front brakes. This is to make sure that the brakes can be released time after time without damaging the inner or outer cables.

 **5** The 'noodle' pipe has a nylon insert that provides protection for the cable and also helps prevent friction in this part of the cable run. When new, these pipes have a small amount of grease squirted into them and it's a good idea to check regularly that the cable is still well lubricated. Use a very small amount of waterproof grease and inject it with a grease gun.

 **6** Cables should be measured (it's easiest to use the old cables as a template) and cut using a quality cable cutter. Make sure that the ends of the cable are flat – they can be tidied up with a metal file – and that the inner nylon part is open at the ends.

 **7** Unlike gear cables, it is only necessary to add a ferrule where the cable will contact the frame stops. The V-brake noodle has its own built-in ferrule. New brake cables usually have a factory-fitted ferrule on one end – I always start with this one at the lever adjuster.

 **KNOW HOW**

Over-long cables

Over-long cables will usually add friction and absorb braking power, so keep the cable lengths to a minimum without sacrificing movement in the handlebars and suspension systems. You should replace the nylon noodle insert if it is damaged, and oil and replace cables regularly.

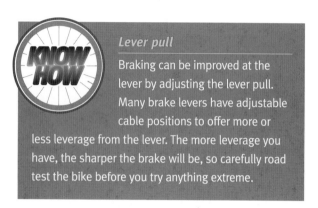

Lever pull

Braking can be improved at the lever by adjusting the lever pull. Many brake levers have adjustable cable positions to offer more or less leverage from the lever. The more leverage you have, the sharper the brake will be, so carefully road test the bike before you try anything extreme.

8 The rear brake cable must be precision-cut so that the curve of the cable is unhindered and smooth. Over-long cables flap about and create friction and can also catch passing undergrowth. However, short cables will pull on the callipers and potentially de-centralise them over the rims.

9 Cable doughnuts are used to prevent the cable slapping on the top tube and wearing out the paintwork (the noise of flapping cables is also highly annoying!). Some people use plastic sleeves instead; however, quality cables are usually made from stainless steel and do not have to be covered, while plastic sleeves can help retain moisture, which will eventually corrode the cables.

10 The gaiter covers the cable as it exits the noodle and prevents any water and mud getting into the noodle pipe. They are not essential and the brake will work perfectly well without them. However, the noodle is the weak link in the V-brake system and needs constant care. It's always worth stripping and re-lubricating the noodle after wet rides.

11 Thread the cable through the fixing bolt and pull the callipers together with the cable. Fasten the inner cable into the calliper using a 5 mm Allen key. Leave 50–60 mm of cable to allow for further adjustment and cut the cable with a sharp cable cutter.

12 Lastly, add a cable-end cap to prevent the cable from fraying. This will prevent injury and enable you to make further adjustments to the brakes.

Road bike brakes - general adjustments

Cable-operated calliper brakes are the lightest, easiest solution to road bike braking, here's how to keep them running smoothly...

Calliper release systems

Backing off the brakes to remove wheels

Road bike brake callipers have improved enormously over the past decade. Dual pivot brakes are designed to allow increased efficiency at the wheel so that the rider's input at the lever is maximised at the rim. In simple terms, a series of linked levers over two pivots apply greater braking pressure.

Brakes need good braking surfaces and true wheels to work properly. Buckled wheels and damaged old rims in poor condition are not only unsafe but will also hinder your riding enjoyment. Braking should be easy and effortless, so if you are putting more effort into 'stopping' than you are into 'going', you should pay some careful attention to your brakes and ensure that your wheels are in good order too. All road brakes have a facility that allows you to back off the brakes in order

Campagnolo have placed the QR on the brake lever.

Shimano brakes use a small lever on the brake itself, next to the fixing bolts.

to be able to remove the wheels – the loosening of the brake calliper allows the tyre to pass easily through the brake pads.

1 On Campagnolo brakes, the small aluminium button on the inside of the lever needs to be depressed before the wheels can be removed.

2 Once released, this will back off the levers and release the pads away from the wheel rim. Remember to return the lever button before riding.

 On Shimano brakes, the QR lever is on the callipers. This is the lever in the 'open' position.

 And this is the QR in the 'closed', ready-to-ride position.

Fixing the callipers to the bike

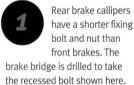 Rear brake callipers have a shorter fixing bolt and nut than front brakes. The brake bridge is drilled to take the recessed bolt shown here.

2 Fit a star washer in between the brake and the frame to secure the calliper and prevent the brake from loosening under normal conditions.

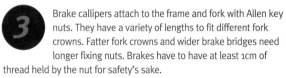

3 Brake callipers attach to the frame and fork with Allen key nuts. They have a variety of lengths to fit different fork crowns. Fatter fork crowns and wider brake bridges need longer fixing nuts. Brakes have to have at least 1cm of thread held by the nut for safety's sake.

4 Install the wheels and tighten the calliper fixing bolts while squeezing the pads onto the rim. This will roughly centre the brake over the rims and allow you to install the cables and adjust the brake pads.

5 Centreing the brakes makes the most of the braking efficiency and prevents the pads from rubbing on the rim. The brakes will also respond faster and feel better at the lever when accurately centred.

6 Shimano brakes can be centred without disturbing the brake fixing bolt. The adjustment screw on the top of the brake allows for fine tuning and perfect alignment.

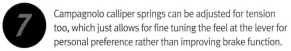

7 Campagnolo calliper springs can be adjusted for tension too, which just allows for fine tuning the feel at the lever for personal preference rather than improving brake function.

8 SRAM callipers use a smaller 10mm spanner to centre the brake pads over the rim. When using a spanner like this always double-check that the fixing bolt is still tight in the frame/fork after adjusting.

Braking

When you brake, no matter which brake you use, your weight is forced forward on the front wheel leaving the back with very little traction. The front brake, then, is the one which will stop you fastest and most safely. Of course, most of us don't use it hard when we start to ride because of the real fear of going over the bars; we use the back brake, which skids out and snakes around with no weight on it. To stop quickly, experiment carefully with putting your weight back, bracing your arms and putting two thirds of the force through the front brake. Don't do this on a slippery surface, on a bumpy surface or if you have had a flat front tyre.

REPAIR & MAINTENANCE
Brake pad alignment

Getting your brake pads lined up perfectly makes all the difference to your ride

The key to brake pad alignment is to have a perfectly central brake calliper and to line up the pads perfectly to the rim, so as to prevent the pad from rubbing against the tyre and to prevent uneven wear to the surface of the pad. Shimano brake systems have a lot of brute force available and are perhaps the easiest to set up.

1 Campagnolo's pad system features a domed washer, which allows you to toe-in the pad and adjust the angle of the pad in relation to the rim.

2 Toe-in prevents the brakes from squealing and improves performance. The pad has to hit the rim at the front of the block first.

3 Pad alignment is equally important in relation to the braking surface and to make sure that the pad clears the tyres. Friction on the tyre can cause damage to the sidewalls.

4 Campagnolo's latest Record Skelton callipers now use Torx headed nuts on their brake fittings.

5 SRAM adopt a similar system to both Campagnolo and Shimano. The adjustment of the pads is similar to Campagnolo's and the cartridge pad system more like Shimano's.

REPAIR & MAINTENANCE
Fitting cartridge brake pads

The stronger, stiffer, one-time solution to braking

Cartridge brake shoes are a better option than totally replaceable brake pads. They are stronger (stiffer) than all-rubber replaceable pads and they can stay in place, and therefore don't need to be adjusted after the pads have been replaced. Over-slack cables and extra movement at the lever may mean that the pads have started to wear. You can adjust cable tension 'on the fly' using the adjusters on the brakes. Long-term adjustment of the slack in a cable system is best done by pulling the cable through at the brake cable fastening bolt on the calliper, and all brake pads have a wear-line indicator that should be checked regularly, especially after long periods of wet weather riding.

1 Campagnolo pads require a very small amount of light grease or Vaseline smeared into the cartridge slot to help the pads slide into place.

2 Position the opening and the pad in the slot. There is a left and right pad and a left- and right-facing cartridge, so before you start make sure that you have the pads and cartridges aligned correctly.

3 Force the brake pad into place, they're supposed to be a tight fit. The open end of the cartridge should always face back so the rotation of the wheel will force the pad against the closed shoulder rather than push it out.

4 Shimano pads have a screw that retains the pad in the cartridge.

 They will slide in and out very easily once this screw is loosened.

Carbon fibre rims

Carbon fibre rim-braking can be problematic – due to its grippy, uneven surface texture, it can't offer the same predictable braking offered by a machined-smooth aluminium rim. The reputation is basically 'all or nothing' and, in the wet, it's often nothing. Do not use standard rubber compound brake pads, as they will grab at the rims, set up dangerous vibrations and even lock the wheels completely. You should always look to use the brand of pad that the wheel manufacturer recommends. Cork compounds from Zipp, Shimano and Swissstop can improve braking. Although never as good as aluminium rims, when fitted with the correct pads they can at least provide predictable and safe stopping.

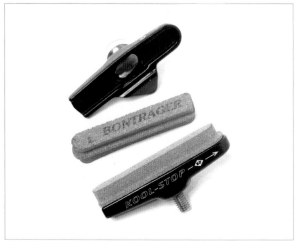

REPAIR & MAINTENANCE
Cable replacement

Neglecting brake cables turns them into the weak link in the system

Road and MTB cable brakes have much in common, but they are not the same, so forgive us while we recap what we said under V-brakes. Your cables are vulnerable so take care of them when removing the wheels and packing the bike for travel. Damaged cables and water inside the cable outers will slow your braking down. A sloppy or stiff feeling in the lever tells you that the inner wire is kinked. Replacing the cable run is the best way to solve this, but stripping out the inner and using a quality spray lube can be a short-term fix.

It's pretty rare for a brake cable to fray dangerously, but it's worth checking the inner cable, especially if the brakes are feeling stiffer than usual. Is there a notchy brake feel? This can also signify that the brake cables have been badly installed, as this added friction is usually caused by the inner cable rubbing on either a burr at the end of the outer cable or a damaged frame cable stop. It's also rare for cables to snap, but they can fray at the clamp bolts, which can make future adjustment difficult.

A slack feeling at the lever with a slow lever return may also mean that the cables need replacing. With cheaper brakes this may also signify the brake springs and pivots have seized.

1 All systems require the cable outer to enter the rear of the brake lever. Make sure that the cable has been neatly cut and there are no sharp edges on the inside.

2 Shimano STI lever housings bury the cable nipple retainer deep inside the lever housing. Flick the lever to one side to allow the lever to fall further forwards and allow easy access.

3 Once the inner cable is in place the grommet can be returned to its position in the lever housing.

KNOW HOW

Cables

Brake cables stretch and become tired, they carry dirt and grit into the outer with them and wear, they kink, they make your brakes feel slack and hard to pull on and then they stop the levers returning quickly. They're not expensive. Change them regularly.

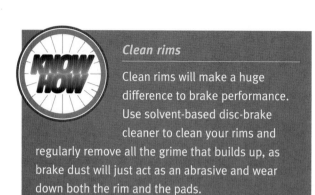

Clean rims

Clean rims will make a huge difference to brake performance. Use solvent-based disc-brake cleaner to clean your rims and regularly remove all the grime that builds up, as brake dust will just act as an abrasive and wear down both the rim and the pads.

4 Campagnolo cables feature a sharp uncut end that makes it very easy to thread the inner wire through the lever.

5 SRAM brake cabling is very similar to Campagnolo's (although it is slightly easier to install).

6 Greasing the brake cable nipple will prevent friction and stop any noises developing as the levers are applied, and it prevents wear and tear on the cable around the nipple too.

7 Measure your new cables against the old ones as a template and cut using a cable cutter. Make sure the ends of the cable are flat – they can be tidied up with a metal file – and that the inner nylon part is open at the ends.

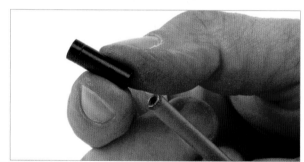

8 New brake cables usually have a factory-fitted ferrule on one end – I always start with this one at the lever adjuster. It's only necessary to add a brake cable ferrule where it will contact the frame stop.

5 The rear brake cable must be precision-cut so that the curve of the cable is unhindered and smooth. Overlong cables flap about and create friction. However, short cables will pull on the callipers and potentially de-centralise them over the rims.

6 Cable doughnuts are used to prevent the cable slapping on the top tube and wearing out the paintwork (the noise of flapping cables is also highly annoying).

8 Do use a cable-end cap to prevent the cable from fraying. This will prevent injury (the ends can be very sharp) and enable you to make further adjustments to the brakes.

7 Thread the inner cable through the fixing bolt and pull the callipers together onto the rim . Fasten the inner cable into the calliper using a 5mm Allen key. Leave 20–30mm of cable to allow for further adjustment, and cut the cable with a sharp cable cutter.

Small hands?
Make sure you can really wrap your hands around the levers

- Experiment with the position of the levers on the bars.
- Use a round, shallow drop bar as this will allow you to get closer to the lever.
- Shimano offer an aftermarket converter that can bring the STI lever closer to the bars.
- Don't run the brake cables too tight, as some slack in the braking system will actually allow your hands to wrap around the lever more.

8

Suspension

We are now seeing the first genuine all-terrain bikes

Full suspension was always an obvious path for the mountain bike to follow. Instead of allowing bump forces to throw bike and rider up in the air, suspension limits its action to the wheels, where possible, and damps the process so that the bike eats bumps and continues under full control and in good order.

First efforts bounced around and weighed a lot, but all that is over. Modern suspension is so light and works so well many riders use their full sus rigs for everything. There are many of us, of course, who love the simplicity of a hard tail, but one begins to wonder whether that is because having won our old school skills with such difficulty we're reluctant to let them go for a system that

"Having won their old school skills with such difficulty hardtail fans are reluctant to let them go"

lets anyone ride stuff that once was so awesomely technical.

Platform shocks

The development of shocks which automatically minimised the effect of pedalling input into a suspension

system incidentally saved the simple single pivot design of frame. Multi pivot points and systems that created virtual pivot points had all been developed to stop the energy sapping bobbing of the rear suspension caused by pedal input, but single pivots looked to be on the way out until the platform technology came on the scene. It's been the saving of some classic frame designs.

Mountain bike suspension

Suspension forks have been standard on mountain bikes for 15 years and sweet working rear systems for five or six. Modern suspension is light for what it does and there's hardly an area of MTB riding it hasn't improved...

The basic idea behind mountain bike suspension is to help isolate the rider from small to medium bumps, reducing rider fatigue and enhancing the overall mountain bike experience. Suspension also improves bike control by allowing the two wheels to track the terrain, maintaining traction. So the key is to keep the suspension supple, whatever type of riding you do – if the suspension is too soft, your bike will use up the travel quickly and possibly damage the internals, and if it is too hard it will make the bike bounce off rough stuff like a pogo stick.

In this book we won't be going into the nuances of each particular suspension configuration, as there are too many of them and they are constantly changing in terms of design and setup. So instead we will concentrate on the fundamentals of any suspension setup: damping and spring rate. Damping controls how quickly the shock or fork compresses or rebounds, while the spring rate suspends the rider and determines how much the suspension compresses under the combined weight of the bike and rider.

The majority of mountain bikes are either air or coil sprung. Determining which spring your rear suspension uses is easy as the spring is external, so you will be able to see either a coil spring or an air canister with a Schraeder valve. Suspension forks are trickier as the springs are housed inside the stanchions (upper legs). To identify which system your fork uses, consult the owner's manual or inspect the dials on the fork crown.

Setting the sag
The most important setting on any mountain bike suspension system is the sag. This is the amount by which the suspension compresses under the combined weight of the bike and rider. So you must set the sag before you ride the bike and check it regularly for optimum performance. Running at 15–25 per cent of the available travel of a fork or shock in sag is essential as this lets the suspension absorb holes as well as bumps, enabling the wheel to hug the ground. The same basic principles apply to forks and shocks, but we will deal with both separately as the techniques for setting the sag vary slightly.

EDITOR'S TIP

"Too much sag means you lower your bottom bracket height and bash rocks with your pedals, but I prefer to start with plenty and firm it up rather than lose any of the benefit. It's trial and error."

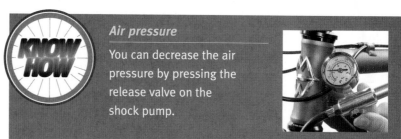

KNOW HOW

Air pressure
You can decrease the air pressure by pressing the release valve on the shock pump.

Setting the 'sag' on forks

If it's going to work properly, suspension needs some sag in the system from the combined weight of bike and rider. Start with the fork...

If there isn't already an O-ring on the stanchion (upper tube), wrap a small zip tie around the leg. Slide this (or the O-ring) down the fork leg until it touches the fork wiper seal.

Prop yourself up against a wall with your elbow, or ask for help to hold the bike upright, and sit on the bike in the normal riding position. If you've compressed the fork a lot when getting on the bike, you will need to reach down and reset the O-ring.

Being careful not to compress the fork further, climb off the bike and measure the sag directly from the fork leg. Sag should be between 15 and 25 per cent of the total travel available, keeping in mind that the total travel will always be slightly less than the amount of stanchion showing.

If you have air-sprung forks, simply increase the air pressure to reduce the amount of sag, or decrease the air pressure to increase the sag.

Coil-sprung forks will normally have a dial on the fork crown that is used to pre-load the spring. If you find that the fork sags too much with the pre-load fully on, you'll need to install a firmer spring. If it sags too little with no pre-load, you'll need to fit a softer spring.

When the sag is set correctly, if you find that the fork bottoms out more than a couple of times every time you ride, you'll need to increase the compression damping. If the fork does not have adjustable compression damping, your only option will be to increase the spring rate (steps 4 and 5).

FAQ: *Which is best: conventional or air-sprung suspension systems?*

They both have their uses. Air is lighter and you can alter the spring rate very easily with a shock pump; coil springs are reliable and plush, but more fiddly to set up. You will find general cross-country riders find air sufficient and big terrain riders are more likely to prefer coil springs.

Setting up the coil sprung rear shock

The coil spring is not a one-size-fits-all item, adjustment will probably do the job, but you may need a different spring...

1 Wind off the compression and rebound damping adjusters. In the fully open position the shock should rebound quickly and compress easily.

2 Unscrew the pre-load collar to the point just before the spring starts to rattle. Then wind it back two full turns.

3 Read the number on the side of the spring to find the spring rate. This is measured in pounds per inch, so a spring rate of 450 lb means that it takes a force of 450 lb to compress the spring by 1 inch.

4 Measure the sag. The easiest way to do this is to first measure the unweighted eye-to-eye distance of the shock. Next, sit on the saddle in normal riding gear and measure the weighted eye-to-eye distance. Subtracting the second measurement from the first will tell you how much the shock has compressed.

5 Typically, sag should measure one quarter to one third of the entire shock stroke. So, a shock with a 2-inch stroke should have approximately half to two thirds of an inch in sag. Too much sag and you need a heavier spring (bigger number); too little and you'll need a lighter spring (smaller number). Dial in the rebound and compression adjusters. Note that the settings will be different if you have changed the weight of the spring.

Tips

✔ If you are running on minimum pre-load, wrap a piece of insulation or PTFE tape around the threads of the shock body as shown in the photograph to stop the pre-load collar backing off.

✔ Rotate the spring so that its tail isn't on the open section of the C-clip, as this can cause the spring to click.

✔ Replacement springs don't come cheap, but some service centres offer exchanges at reduced rates.

Setting up the air sprung rear shock

This is where you appreciate the simplicity of air; all you need is a good shock pump and a zip tie...

1 A good starting point for any air shock is your body weight in pounds. So, if you weigh 150 lb, inflate the positive air chamber to 150 PSI.

2 Push the shock O-ring up the shock body so that it butts up against the air canister.

3 Propping yourself up against a wall with your elbow, sit on the bike in your normal riding position. Now reach down and re-set the O-ring.

4 Being careful not to compress the shock further, climb off the bike and measure the sag directly from the shock body.

5 Run between 15 and 25 per cent of the available travel in sag. So, if your shock has a 1/2-inch stroke, start with 3/8 inch in sag. Inflate the shock to reduce the amount of sag or reduce the air pressure to increase the sag – it's that easy. As with forks, if you find that you bottom the shock easily, increase the air pressure and reduce the amount of sag. Alternatively, if the shock has a compression damping adjustment, increase the compression damping to prevent the shock from bottoming.

UPGRADE...
Tubeless Tyres (MTB)
For a little more installation effort, tubeless MTB tyres are both lighter and less prone to punctures than clincher tyres.

KNOW HOW

Rear suspension unit

Whatever design you prefer, your bike's suspension system is only as good as the elements that control the travel and the response to trail conditions. The latest generation of shocks are now 'trail sensitive' in that they are controlled by rider input to the pedals and weight distribution across the bike, rather than the rider having to fiddle with knobs and dials. Remote lockout levers have made cross-country suspension bikes climb hills without bobbing or soaking up energy, and they are fast becoming the top choice for Enduro riders and racers. Rear shocks are sealed units and are best serviced by experts, so send them away to those who know best as some require compression and specialist tooling to get them apart.

Fine tuning & adjusting suspension

Suspension doesn't just isolate the mass of bike and rider from bump forces on the wheels, it can alter bike geometry and ride feel too...

The amount of sag you run affects the geometry of the bike. So, if you find that the bottom bracket is too low or the head angle is too slack, run slightly less sag in the rear shock to raise the bottom bracket and steepen the head and vice versa.

If you're riding steep, technical terrain where the switchbacks drop away suddenly, you may want to increase the spring rate in the fork. This reduces the amount of sag so that you ride higher in the travel. Not only will this slacken the head angle slightly, making the bike more stable at speed, but it will also stop the fork from diving as much, making those slow, tight, rocky switchbacks all the easier to clean.

Adjusting the rebound damping

With the sag set, the next step to achieving the perfect suspension setup is to fine-tune the rebound damping. While air and coil springs suspend the rider, it's the oils

and valves inside the shock that control the energy released by the spring. Specifically, rebound damping controls how fast the shock or fork returns (rebounds) to the sag position. Too much damping and the suspension will return slowly and won't be ready for the next hit; not enough damping causes the suspension to spring back uncontrollably.

Shocks and forks have a massive range of adjustment so it is very easy to get the rebound setting wrong. And because the majority of weight on a full suspension bike is supported by the rear suspension, it is the most important thing to get right. With the sag sorted and the rebound adjuster fully out, ride off a medium-sized kerb in the seated position. You should be able to feel the shock oscillating about the sag position beneath you on impact. Increase the rebound damping by a click and repeat. When the shock settles to the sag position within two cycles, you're ready to ride.

As a rule, less rebound damping makes the bike springier and increases the sensitivity of the suspension to small bumps, while increasing the rebound damping stops the bike bucking on drops and big hits but reduces some of the sensitivity. The steps outlined above are just a guideline to get you started. If you find that on the trail the bike bucks too much and feels uncontrolled, gradually increase the rebound damping. On the other hand, if the suspension seems to pack down and isn't responsive to smaller bumps, reduce the amount of rebound damping. It's also worth noting that suspension feedback into the drivetrain is less noticeable with increased damping. Ultimately, there is no ideal setting, so experiment and find out what works best for you.

Platform damping

Platform damping can affect the sag setting, so if you make changes to your level of platform damping – especially if it's controlled by the internal floating piston (IFP) pressure as found on Manitou and Progressive shocks – always check the sag. Some shocks have bodies that are considerably longer than the stroke of the shock. This can lead to a false sag reading, so always deflate the shock then fully compress it to determine the true shock stroke.

CARE & MAINTENANCE
Looking after your suspension fork

Fork internals are best left to a specialist, but like other moving parts on a bicycle they benefit from cleaning and lubrication.

Anatomy of a suspension fork

1. Steerer tube

The steerer tube is a butted aluminium or steel threadless tube that connects the fork to the frame via the headset and is usually 1 1/8 inch in diameter. One Point Five is an oversized head tube/fork standard that allows manufacturers to make lightweight long-travel single crown forks without compromising strength.

2. Crown

Fork crowns are forged or cast and are often hollow to save weight. The steerer tube is normally press-fitted into the crown, as are the stanchions (see below).

3. Stanchions

All telescopic suspension forks have stanchions (upper tubes). Diameters vary from 28.6 mm on XC forks to 40 mm on some downhill forks. Aluminium is the favoured material to keep weight down, and stanchions normally have a hardened surface coating to reduce stiction and wear.

4. Dust seals

Also called wiper seals, these are the primary defence in keeping contaminants out of the forks. The improved quality of dust seals has made boots redundant.

5. Oil seals

These are hidden beneath the dust seals and keep the oil inside the fork.

6. Bushings

Most forks have upper and lower bushings (bearings) in each leg to guide the stanchions into the lowers.

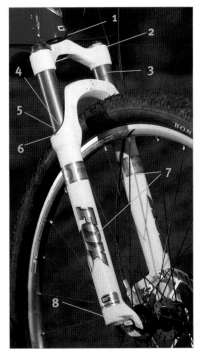

7. Lowers

Normally cast from magnesium to minimise un-sprung mass, the fork lowers are the bits that have to move up and down over the bumps and include the brace, which prevents the fork legs from moving independently.

8. Dropout

This is where the wheel is secured. The dropouts can be either quick release or 20 mm bolt-through.

KNOW HOW

Front fork with lockout

Front suspension has been a regular fixture on mountain bikes for the last ten years, and it's actually pretty rare to see a bike with rigid forks these days. Like rear suspension units, the new style of fork is far more sophisticated and, as with most high-tech mountain bike components, servicing them is more prevention than cure.

CARE & MAINTENANCE
Built-in seal lubrication

The semi-bath lubrication system is associated with Manitou forks but found on others too

Most riders neglect their forks, but the suspension is a moving part that is exposed to the elements so regular cleaning and lubrication are essential. Just like the drivetrain, neglect will cause premature wear and diminished performance, often resulting in irreparable damage.

Fork maintenance

As with any moving part, fork maintenance consists of cleaning and lubrication. So, after every ride clean the stanchions and wiper seals, paying particular attention to the area between the fork brace and the seal. Add a drop of oil and massage it in by pumping the forks a few times.

Manitou has recently switched to a Semi-bath lubrication system with 16 cc of oil slopping around in each of the lower legs to keep everything running smoothly. Over time, the oil breaks down and eventually weeps out through the wiper seals. Here's how to top up the lube in these forks.

1 On forks with rapid travel adjust or wind-down, make sure that you switch the travel to the longest setting. Then turn the bike upside down, exposing the bottom of the fork lowers. Using a 2mm Allen key, remove any adjusters (making a note of their orientation) and place to one side.

2 If the fork does not have a rapid travel adjuster, you will see an 11 mm bolt at the bottom of the left leg (rider's perspective). Remove this bolt, turning it anti-clockwise.

3 Insert an 8 mm Allen key into the right leg (rider's perspective) but do not unscrew it. The Allen head is attached directly to the rebound damper shaft and must be screwed into the fork (clockwise) to release the lowers.

4 Slide the lowers up by about 2 inches to disengage the damper and spring shafts. Using a syringe, inject 16 cc of Semi-bath oil into each leg.

5 Press the lower legs down onto the inner leg assembly (stanchions) until the damper shafts make contact with the casting. Using the 8 mm Allen key, turn the damper shaft anti-clockwise into the lower leg.

6 Install the damper rod and adjuster if applicable. Install the spring rod bolt and torque to 2–3 Nm using an 11 mm socket. Install the rapid travel adjuster if applicable. Upright the bike and check that the forks function as normal.

CARE & MAINTENANCE
Looking after your wiper seals

Demonstrated using a Fox fork, this is a procedure Fox recommends

1 Use a small flat-blade screwdriver to pry the seals from the lower legs of the fork. Fox recommends that the tip of the screwdriver be covered with tape to protect the paint on the fork. I go further and wrap clean rags around the stanchions to prevent scratching.

2 Once the seals are loose, remove the rags and slide the seals all the way up to the crown. Take the same rags and wrap them around the junction of the upper and lower legs to stop dirt getting into the fork.

3 Use another rag to clean the outside edge of the seals. Remove all the dirt and inspect the seals for damage like cracks or scratches in the surface.

4 Remove the rags from the fork legs and inspect the foam O-rings in-side the lower legs.

5 The seals should be free of dirt and soaked in oil. If the foam O-rings are dry, use a few drops of Fox suspension fluid to soak them. Then wipe the upper tubes clean and slide the seals back down onto the lower legs.

6 Press the seals in using a large, covered flat-blade screwdriver, starting between the fork brace and the stanchions and working your way around to the back of the fork.

7 Check that the seals are firmly seated against the fork lowers and cycle the fork several times to check that everything is okay.

KNOW HOW

Storage

Store your bike upside down to keep the upper bushing and foam O-ring soaked in oil, ready for your next ride. But remember to cycle the fork several times when you upright the bike to recharge the damper with oil.

CARE & MAINTENANCE
Looking after your rear shock

Look at the linkages on your rear shock and you'll see how much there is to wear out...

If you've got a full suspension bike, it doesn't take long to figure out that with all those moving parts something is bound to wear out. Invariably, the first thing to go is the DU bushing – that's the small collar in either end of the shock. Virtually all rear shocks, regardless of whether or not they are air- or coil-sprung, are fixed to the frame using DU bushings and aluminium fitting

hardware. Shock manufacturers like Manitou, Fox, RockShox and Progressive Suspension all use universal eyelet dimensions and the bushings are designed to be perishable so that the inexpensive bushing wears, rather than expensive shock unit.

Shock and rider location both determine how quickly the bushing will wear out. On the whole, the bushings on shocks that are

Tools:
- Allen keys
- 10mm spanner
- DU bushing tool

positioned in front of the seat tube last longer, as they are not in the firing line of mud being flung off the rear wheel. Also, if you live in a dry, dusty climate, chances are that the bushings could last for years.

Checking for and replacing a worn bushing

1 Before rushing out to buy the necessary tools and replacement bushings, check that the shock mounting bolts are actually tight. If you discover a bolt that isn't fully tightened, remove it, apply a small amount of Loctite to the threads and refit it.

2 With the shock secured, apply a small amount of downward pressure on the back portion of the saddle, then lift the saddle up ever so slightly, keeping the rear wheel on the ground at all times.

3 If there is a small knock, similar to a loose headset, then one or both of the bushings are worn. If you watch the bushings while rocking the saddle you should be able to see the movement and determine which one needs replacing.

4 Remove the shock from the frame using the appropriate Allen keys or spanners.

> **Warning!** Do not attempt to dismantle shock units at home, as most shocks are charged with gas and dismantling them could result in serious injury. Always have your shock serviced at an authorised service centre. And, as always: read the manual!

5 If the DU bushing is worn, you should have no problem removing the alloy shock mounts. If they don't come out easily, clamp them in the soft jaws of a vice and wiggle them out. All Fox bushings are supplied with new fitting kits as both items tend to wear together, so don't worry about damaging the old hardware.

6 Slide the thin end of the male portion of the bushing tool through the shock eyelet.

7 Next, slide the tapered end of the female portion of the tool over the thin end of the male tool.

8 Place both ends of the tool in a vice and slowly compress until the worn bushing pops out.

9 Now, place a fresh bushing onto the thin end of the male tool and flip the female portion of the tool over so that the tapered end is in contact with the vice. Press in the new bushing.

10 Fit the new shock spacers and re-install the shock.

Tips

✔ When unbolting the shock, support the frame (or the rear wheel if the bike is in a stand) to stop the bike collapsing or overextending as this could damage the shock or frame. An old toe strap is good for this.

✔ Fit small O-rings between the DU bushings and fitting hardware to reduce dirt build-up. If you grease the bushing, wipe away any excess grease. Have your shock serviced annually to maximise performance and longevity.

Troubleshooting

What can go wrong with your fork and shock and what to do about it...

Fork problems

The fork is rocking

Check that the headset is tight, as the bushing may be worn. Have the fork inspected by a professional suspension-tuning centre.

The fork is topping out

Increase the rebound damping. If this doesn't cure the problem, the internals may be damaged.

The fork is bottoming out

The spring rate may be too soft, or there may be insufficient compression damping. If the sag is correct then you need to increase the damping.

The fork feels harsh

The spring could be too firm, or you may have too much compression damping resulting in a 'spike'. If the fork doesn't have an external compression adjuster, try using a lighter-weight oil in the fork.

The fork rebounds too quickly

Increase the rebound damping and, if the fork doesn't have an external rebound adjuster, try using a lighter-weight oil in the fork, assuming that the fork isn't friction damped.

After compression the fork takes ages to return to the sag position

Completely back off the rebound damping and, if that doesn't cure the problem, get it checked out at an authorised service centre.

The fork action is notchy

This is probably due to stiction (static friction). Strip and clean the fork as per the manufacturer's instructions, or have it serviced at a recognised service centre.

Shock problems

The shock is losing air

Check that the valve body is tight in the air canister and that the valve core is also tight.

The shock is topping out

Increase the amount of rebound damping. If the shock still tops out, take it to an authorised dealer for inspection.

There is an excessive amount of oil on the shock shaft (coil) or body (air)

Clean and inspect the seal. If the leaking persists, the shock will need servicing.

My shock is making slurping noises

The oil has become emulsified, that is gas and oil are mixed together, which will result in inconsistent damping. Return the shock for a service.

The shock is packed down

Wind the rebound damping fully off (anti-clockwise). If this does not cure the problem, have the shock inspected at a service centre.

EDITOR'S TIP *"Don't be too overawed by shock and suspension technology, it's all very clever but basically you're looking at a can of air controlled by a tube of oil and a stack of washers on a stick."*